W9-AXR-190

The No-Fear Career

12 Steps to Becoming a
Courageous Leader in the
Face of Uncertainty

Robin Fisher Roffer

Library of Congress Cataloging-in-Publication Data:
Roffer, Robin Fisher,
The No-Fear Career: 12 Steps to Becoming a Courageous Leader in the Face of Uncertainty / Robin Fisher Roffer.

    1. Success in business. 2. Success. 3. Career development. 4. Self-realization.

There are two basic motivating forces: fear and love. When we are afraid, we pull back from life. When we are in love, we open to all that life has to offer with passion, excitement and acceptance. We need to learn to love ourselves first, in all our glory and imperfections.

— John Lennon

Contents

Introduction

The office can be a scary place. There are demanding clients, bosses who bully, conniving co-workers, and people who play politics. It seems that fear, mistrust, anxiety and feeling overwhelmed run through the veins of professionals at every level. When left unchecked, this fear creates a negative work environment that stifles innovation and sabotages service – the very things needed to gain a competitive edge.

The flip side of fear is faith. When we have faith, we simply can't be in fear. But how do we have faith in our company and in ourselves when demands are coming at us so fast and the future seems so uncertain?

With the speed of business advancing at such a high rate, what feels like a groundbreaking idea today can be seen as old age thinking by tomorrow. Running on a hamster wheel, we try to find our place in the fastest changing market the world has ever known. Unfortunately, many of us don't have the ability to thrive on change, so we go round and round until we become irrelevant and discarded.

We're afraid of getting hurt. We're afraid of rejection. We're afraid we are too old. We're afraid we are too young. We're afraid we will be criticized. We're afraid that we are under appreciated. We're afraid we are in over our head. We're afraid we're not enough. I say "we" because I have yet to run across a professional that hasn't felt these fears. The courageous among us don't get stuck asking, "Why is this happening to me?" They accept what is and move forward fearlessly.

Ironically, the more I write and lecture on the art of being fearless, the more I find myself in situations that scare me to death.

I'm not talking about jumping out of airplanes or crossing the border into North Korea – the things I do are fearless on another level. For example, I left my Midwest hometown of Cleveland, Ohio to go to the Deep South and attend the University of Alabama. I made a name for myself at Turner Networks as a Media-Marketing Specialist helping to launch TNT and turn CNN into "The World's News Leader." Then I chucked my corporate job and started my own marketing firm - Big Fish - reinventing it many times over the last 20 years so that it remained relevant and profitable. After building the multimillion-dollar online advertising division of my LA-based company, I dissolved it and relocated my family and business to Santa Fe, New Mexico.

Today I work with big brands and top executives on messaging, marketing and corporate strategies. I also give keynote speeches to large audiences and lead workshops that bring people with different points of view to the same page. Most of my clients see what I do as nothing short of death-defying acts. For me, being on that edge is where I feel most alive.

If you want a big career, you have to put yourself out there. When you do, you're bound to bump up against fear. In my case, I face it with a fair amount of chutzpah and a whole lot of drive. I choose to push through because I know I want what's on the other side.

I frequently facilitate meetings with the world's most powerful executives from companies like Sony, FOX, Food Network, Walmart, Mattel, and Microsoft. What I've found is that from the C-suite to the folks that answer the phone, no one is immune from fear. To combat fear, I unite and galvanize companies behind a unique mission and vision that gives them the courage to keep moving forward. I arrive when companies are ready to make a bold leap forward or feel rudderless because there has been a huge shift in the market. I am there to keep my clients on the right track and to help them find their North Star.

In this book I share the tried and true tools and methodology I use with these corporate giants. Whether you're in fashion or dentistry, the CEO of a huge firm or a recent graduate, the fear is the same. This book will help you not only survive, but thrive in the face of uncertainty. These 12-steps will inspire you to find the courage to reach your highest potential as a professional or business owner. Loaded with actionable takeaways, you'll be able to apply what you learn to your business, your personal life, and your community so that you can approach any situation fearlessly.

I've written this book in bite sized, blog-like sections so you can absorb it quickly. However, there is no need to rush through it. Take each step as it comes. I suggest you get create a journal on your laptop or in a notebook so you can work on the exercises and map your progress. If you own this book, mark it up and keep it as a reference. Challenge yourself to take risks and answer all the questions I pose truthfully. This book is for you to use as a toolbox with the instruments needed to help you get your swagger on, keep your cool in front of key influencers, and let go of everything that is holding you back.

Uncovering and trusting your authentic self is the key to finding a lion-like nature that will catapult you to what's next. Like eating an artichoke, you'll have to peel leaf by leaf to get to the heart.

Whether you are about to jumpstart your own business, are ready to climb the next step on the corporate ladder, have lost your job and your mojo, or are just entering the job market and want to stand out from millions of other applicants, this book is exactly what you need.

I invite you to come to this text willing to do the groundwork. Once you get started, you will be surprised by how many doors will open for you. So lean forward, listen up, and dive in. In front of you is the key to unlock your No-Fear Career.

Step 1:
Own Your Truth

Today, people who rise to the top in business own their truth and live their lives with conviction. It begins with knowing who you are and what you value by peeling away the layers and demonstrating compassion for yourself and others.

In this step you will learn to:

Accept Your Flaws

Uncover the Real You

Work From Needs vs. Wants

Celebrate Your Differences

Put First Things First

Get on a Mission

Accept Yourself And Others Will Follow

Authenticity isn't about telling the truth as much as owning it.

Diane Arbus once said, "A photograph is a secret about a secret. The more it tells you the less you know." A few years ago my sister sent me an old photograph that contained a myriad of secrets.

The picture is taken in Hot Springs, California, where we are living in a trailer park. I am 5 years old and I'm holding a white poodle puppy. My little sister Wendy is seated next to me. We are wearing matching red pants. My grandmother is smoking a cigarette in a red housecoat. A white haired woman I don't recognize stands behind us with clenched fists.

At the time the photograph is taken, my grandmother is an alcoholic. I remember feeling terrified and hungry when we stayed with her. Yet despite our situation, I try to act happy for the camera. Later in business, I will use this survival skill to receive promotions and keep clients loyal. It will serve me well – until it doesn't.

Everyone is talking about being authentic. But what does it mean? What does authenticity even look like?

For years I hid these secrets. I wore the mask of someone who had it all together and held all the answers. I was desperate to break free of my past. I was ashamed of the poverty I had grown up in and the circumstances that eventually led to my mother losing custody of us. So I covered them up with beautiful clothes and built a business based on cultivating an ideal brand image.

Eventually, I would come to view my past as a gift. I would own that I am scared of things that feel out of my control and stop apologizing for my need to have everything in its place.

It took a long time, but I have learned that it's okay not to agree with everyone. It hurt at first, but it got easier to say "no" when people were taking advantage of me. Soon I could tell my truth and not stand in judgment of the reaction. This was being me, authentically.

How do you honor who you are and show up authentically when you're just trying to hold on to what you've got?

It's not easy being certain about yourself in an uncertain world. But if you keep denying the truth about you and you don't own the beauty of your uniqueness, you'll never feel whole.

So… if museums bore you, don't go. If you like to drink whiskey more than wine, then ask for it. Stop camping if you hate it. If Christmas isn't your thing, don't celebrate it. If you have a friend that's driving you crazy, don't call her. Just be you, *really you.*

Consciously be aware of how things make you feel and gravitate towards what and who makes you feel good. You'll find that some relationships are strengthened by your authenticity. Others are weakened. Not everyone will love the real you. What matters is that you do.

I am the little girl in the picture – there's no denying it. I survived my childhood and because of it (not in spite of it), I am thriving as an adult. People who are rising to the top in business tell their truth and live their lives with conviction. They own their past, let go of old patterns, exhibit faith and show compassion for themselves and others.

Many of my friends who are tuned into universal shifts say that there is a new paradigm happening. And as a result, those who exhibit fear, put on false personas or hide behind masks of the martyr, worker bee, people pleaser, jerk, tough cookie, creep – fill in the blank – are finding themselves out of step with the transformation taking place.

In an Age of Transparency, authenticity is the only answer. It's the fuel to forgive what was and move with grace into what's next.

So You're Flawed, Who Isn't?

To step away from fear, you have to accept what's different about you.

For as long as I can remember, I've always been self-conscious about my prominent Jewish nose. So naturally, I protested when Mark Hanauer, a well-known LA-based photographer, made me turn sideways to shoot my profile. The result is one of the best photos ever taken of me.

When I posted that picture on my Facebook page I asked my friends what they could love about themselves, that up until now, they had viewed as a negative. I received an avalanche of responses. It was very affirming for me – an unexpected and superb gift.

Whether it's Jay Leno's iconic chin, Madonna's gapped teeth, Beyonce's curvaceous booty, or the fact that Barbara Walters can't pronounce the letter "R", having a distinctive "flaw" can be something to celebrate and turn into an important feature of your personal brand.

Think about how you can turn your "flaw" into the thing that makes you unique.

Courageous leaders distinguish themselves from the rest of the crowd. I'm not talking about being shocking; rather, I'm talking about being unforgettable in an authentic way. That type of presence comes from the inner knowledge that you're okay just the way you are.

So often we are too apologetic for our shortcomings, when we should be accepting, even celebrating ourselves – warts and all. If you are hard on yourself, others will be hard on you. If you come from a place of strength, your relationships will be strong. The truth is people can only accept you as much as you can accept yourself. Every important relationship in your life is a reflection of how you feel about yourself.

It's time to stop apologizing for who you are and open up to your authentic self. To do this, start by freeing yourself from the desire to conform. When we accept ourselves, others follow.

It's time to positively change the way you see yourself.

To illuminate what makes you positively different, take a few minutes to answer these questions:

- Do you look, act or think differently from others?
- Have you had any big challenges at work because you are seen as different?
- Did anything positive come out of the challenge?
- What did you learn about yourself?
- How can you turn what's different about you to your advantage?

The key to developing self-acceptance is acknowledging what is in place, what is working, and having gratitude for that. It's about focusing on what you have instead of harboring a sense of scarcity and always looking at what seems to be wrong with you or what's missing from your life. When you live with the constant feeling that you don't have enough or that you are not enough, others will see you that way.

By appreciating your true nature, you can overcome any fears that stop you from seeing yourself as an extraordinary person, just as you are. I'm starting with my nose. What will you celebrate about yourself today that has felt like a flaw? It's time to get comfortable in your own skin – fearlessly knowing that to the degree you accept yourself, the world will accept you as well.

Now that you know what makes you unique, work fearlessly to reflect who you are in all you do.

Needs vs. Wants

Why is it that when we get what we want it can feel like a hollow victory? Maybe it's because we didn't really need it after all.

Life is a process of endings and beginnings. At the end of my marriage I made a list of what I needed and what I wanted in my life. This was soul-searching work. For so long I had operated from a place of want. I bought things because I wanted them. I had that extra glass of wine because I wanted it. I chose partners and projects because I wanted to be wanted. My wants were primal and fleeting.

It was not in my nature to work from a place of need. Even admitting that I needed anything was painful.

I sat and pondered the question, "What do I really need?" I went to my core values of love, safety and integrity. Yes, I needed these values operating in my life, but how did I need them to show up?

Based on my core values, I came up with 5 needs that I would admit to myself:

1. I need to attract partners and clients who understand that I have a daughter and she comes first.
2. I need to surround myself with people and projects that help me grow as a professional and whole person.
3. I need to have my own independent life that involves travel and living everyday as a grand adventure.
4. I need to have a spiritual practice and conscious people in my life who empower me to accept myself as I am.
5. I need to give love and receive love through acceptance, kindness and sensitivity.

The question becomes: if you only focus on what you need, can you still get what you want?

Making a list of my wants was much easier. There was a desire for lucrative clients that provided a steady stream of revenue, tickets and invitations to exciting events, meaningful recognition for my work, beautiful clothes and sophisticated company. After I made my two lists, what I needed started to arrive quickly and many of my wants came along as a bonus.

I have a lot of friends and clients who consistently get what they want. They are powerful people who can manifest their desires. The great job, car, girl or house…it all becomes a prize won, rather than a deep need fulfilled. So the desire for more things increases and the feeling of satisfaction doesn't last. That gaping hole remains along with a feeling of restlessness and envy. Moving into a needs-based motivation simplifies, clarifies and attracts opportunities that are much deeper and more fulfilling. That's my experience. I hope it is yours.

For those who want to live their life on purpose and find fulfillment, declaring what you need is where to begin.

Will The Real YOU Please Stand Up?

It's high time you finally declare your core values and stick to them.

There is no doubt that one of the worst things a leader can be called is a wishy-washy flip-flopper. So isn't it ironic that most of the people doing the name-calling haven't declared their own values or definitively told their employees or customers what they stand for or believe in? Too busy bending the rules or chasing an elusive dream at all costs, they fail to live their lives with conviction. Holding others to a high standard, they themselves are unremarkable.

Your core values are integral to creating boundaries. Knowing what's essential to your soul will help you draw the line.

Successful companies are built on core values and they constantly reinforce those values. They'll illustrate their values in their logo; they'll recite their values in their taglines; they'll promote their values in their public relations efforts.

Effective business leaders sculpt their executive presence by the values they hold dear. What words speak of <u>your</u> personal value system, that metronome for personal behavior—what you stand for, what you want to live up to, what you consider most important to your inner life and well-being?

Quaker Oats products want you to know that they stand for old-fashioned, homespun American goodness. Their logo uses that familiar, friendly-looking Pilgrim to personify those values. Everybody knows that Nike is a synonym for an active lifestyle. Whole Foods announced not long ago that its own line of 365 food products would never contain GMOs. It wants its customers to know where its values lie. Volvo values safety above all, and advertises itself that way.

My values have to do with inspiration, safety, integrity, and love. I feel the absolute best when these four values are operating in my life. I think I'm less than complete when any of them are compromised. I want to stand for these things and be known for them, and so I build these values into my personal brand.

Words that may help you identify what's deeply meaningful in your life could include authenticity, generosity, honesty, success, kindness, loyalty, connection, courage, risk taking, inspiration, wisdom, contentment, knowledge, wealth, security, adventure, justice, freedom, optimism, spirituality and commitment.

Which words do you consider to be your core values? Which three or four values are the most meaningful to you? Which values do you live by? Which would you defend with your dying breath? Core values are also "essential." That is you feel you couldn't live without them. And they are "universal," which means that they apply in all circumstances for you, all the time.

Now ask yourself these two questions: How do I act out my core values every day? And how do I deny my value system?

For example, <u>love</u> is one of my core values. One of the ways I act out that value in my daily life is through my work, which I love; with my daughter, whom I adore; and toward myself, by eating right and working out and keeping healthy. I would be denying these values if I began to take what's so precious to me for granted, got sloppy with my work, ignored my daughter, or stopped taking care of myself. Another of my core values is <u>inspiration</u>, and I act that out by cheerleading my clients and giving myself no limits to meeting my potential. I would be denying this value if I became a hermit, or if I began to act as if there was something more important than showing up in my highest self.

To be seen as a strong leader, one that stands for your beliefs and has a voice that is heard clearly and rings true, you must declare your core values and work everyday not to compromise them. That's because if all is gone tomorrow – if you left your job – shuttered your business or got let go – you'd still know who you are. You'd have your core. You'd have value.

Core values define who you are. If you don't stand up for what you believe in, you won't stand a chance.

Fearlessly Own Your Weirdness

Lady Gaga got it right: "Baby, you were born this way." Your leadership style should celebrate the real you!

Being different is good. That's what I believe. To prove this point, I interviewed dozens of successful professionals who succeeded not despite their differences, but because of them. One by one they built a case for standing out and confirmed my premise that conformity is not distinguishing. What they revealed to me is that people who are at the top of their game shine a light on their uniqueness and fearlessly, authentically move forward. Here are the common threads I found in my interviews and what you can do to follow their lead.

Accept Yourself Without Apology

The first step is to peel away the layers you've piled on in your attempts to fit in. No matter your color, cultural background, or way of seeing the world, it's about becoming comfortable in your own skin and accepting yourself without apology.

Use Your Differences To Positively Stand Out

When you are different, people take a second look at you. You're intriguing. You bring the possibility for change. You inspire curiosity. You attract attention. So why not use your differences to stand out in a positive way?

Find An Anchor In Rough Seas

When you feel like the only one like you, take time to discover who, when, and what you find comfort in so you can anchor yourself in your own uniqueness. Look for other people like you - yes, they do exist - and lead the way for them to become accepted.

Fit In Without Blending In

Instead of fighting the company culture, embrace it without getting lost in it. Be a cultural detective by taking someone who has been at the company a long time to lunch. Ask them to share the history. If you're interviewing for a job or trying to win a client, go online to dig up interesting facts about the company – learning about its mission and its vision. Then, focus on the values that resonate with you.

Make A Difference

Those who are different are perfectly positioned to *make* a difference. It's time to discover that you can create change and be an inspiration because you *don't* blend in. Find your cause and lead the charge!

Reinvent Yourself Over and Over

The way to live deeply is to keep reinventing yourself, changing with the times while holding on to the essential you. It's about staying true to the essence of who you are, and then recasting it to feel brand new.

Practice Your Action, Belief and Courage

Overcome any obstacles that get in your way by practicing your ABCs: Action, Belief, and Courage. Muster the courage to go on by remembering a time when you triumphed, hold that belief in yourself and take action.

The key to celebrating what makes you different is to be yourself – love who you are and be proud of who you are.

I have personally taken these steps and it changed my life. I started out as a follower who operated from fear – someone who sought approval – but I turned it all around and became a leader. I swam against the corporate tide and launched my own business in a male-dominated field. Then I stepped out as an author, public speaker and trainer. With each challenge I could see what I was made of and eventually broke though my feelings of isolation and discomfort. By adhering to this advice, you can overcome that nagging desire to conform and free yourself to live your true purpose.

Striving for a cookie-cutter image and "normal" way of thinking will stamp out your individuality. It's time to step into your power NOW by living honestly.

Get On A Mission

Each of us is born for a specific purpose. Now is the time to uncover your calling to give your life and career real meaning.

Last year I was surfing the web looking for inspiration when I came across Simon Sinek's TED Talk entitled "How Great Leaders Inspire Action." Sinek's premise is that organizations and their leaders create emotional connections and galvanize loyalty when they start with "WHY" they do what they do, rather than drone on about "WHAT" they do or "HOW" they do it.

Think about it. You're most likely to be loyal to brands that have clearly articulated a larger meaning for their existence. Maybe they are on a mission, perhaps even leading a cause or movement. Knowing that a brand wants you to think different (Apple) or just do it (Nike) or experience magic (Disney) draws you in and inspires you.

How often do you start a conversation with WHAT you do, rather than WHY you do it?

Starting with WHY is the key to immediate attraction and engagement. When I tell people that my mission is to "Inspire professionals and their companies to fearlessly achieve their highest potential," they want to know more. My mission serves as a North Star to guide my life and my work – inspiring others and informing everything I do.

If you're wondering why you're not getting the projects or clients you desire, maybe it's because you haven't clearly articulated WHY you do what you do. You haven't given your work a deeper meaning that would inspire action and loyalty.

To uncover your WHY, you have to step back from your life, go inside yourself and quietly ask the question, "Why am I here?" The answer that comes back to you will help you declare your mission and shape how you move forward in your career.

A friend of mine, the great poet and Pakistani businesswoman Syeda Henna Babar Ali, recently shared with me the importance of self-reflection. She said, "The fundamental thing is to know ourselves, to understand ourselves, to be ourselves and to learn to live with ourselves." Those that can do this to optimum capacity thrive because they effortlessly start with WHY.

I believe that we are all one – deeply connected to each other's actions and reactions, but we are not the same. Each one of us has a job to do in his or her lifetime that entails more than punching a clock, putting food on the table and chauffeuring kids. The journey, and what has been the real joy in my life, is to finally find my mission and harness all my energy to it.

Surrender to who you are and WHY you are here. It will be a beautiful and powerful experience to discover the purpose of your life.

Step 2:
Quiet Your Inner Judge

Let go of good and bad, right and wrong, black and white and the person you think you should be. Ask yourself, "Is what I'm obsessing about really important?" This question could save your business and your life.

In this step you will learn to:

Empty the Trash in Your Head

Let Go of Blame and Guilt

Accept Mistakes and Move On

Make Friends With Uncertainty

Practice Compromise and Civility

Emptying The Trash In Your Head

Raising self-esteem starts with letting go of judgment towards others and yourself.

During my twenties, I had been successful in business, but my personal relationships never seemed to last. In fact, I was divorced for the second time by my thirtieth birthday.

I look back on who I was then – a people pleaser, a perfectionist who never felt good enough, and a harsh judge with high expectations. Upon leaving my second marriage, I made a decision to cut the people around me a break and stop beating myself up.

To accomplish this seemingly impossible goal, my friend Kim Youngblood suggested I go to The Esalen Institute in Big Sur (where the human potential movement started in the 1960s), take a workshop, and get on the path to self-awareness.

After combing through their catalogue of workshops focusing on everything from yoga to vision painting to dream analysis to relationships, I chose a weeklong session called "Letting Go and Moving On" with Mary Goldenson.

During this transformational workshop, we were asked to choose our biggest demon, and then talk to it as if it were a person. My demon was "Judgment." There I was, sitting with Judgment (a pillow propped up on a chair), telling it I was hurt by its harsh assessment of my actions. After all, I was just a human with flaws like everyone else. I was tired of Judgment making me feel inadequate—and, at times, worthless. I tried to convince Judgment I was simply different from everyone else – and that if I was understood – I would be loved.

That's when the light bulb went on. Raising my self-esteem, had to start with me. If I accepted myself, others would, too.

In the days that followed, I formed friendships with a few people in the group who encouraged me to open up and share moments in my life that were, until this point, secrets. When they told me their stories, I made myself listen without prejudice and found I liked my new friends, warts and all. Would I be accepted if I came clean?

On the last day of the workshop, I took a chance and spilled everything about my mother's abandoning of me, my lost childhood, and my failure to love anyone fully – including myself. And you know what? I received acceptance. Now I had a chance to do the same for myself. It all came from seeking support from people who were like me—not perfect, and wanting to feel okay about it.

Your inner judge is keeping you from raising self-esteem to achieve success in your work and personal life.

There is so much prejudice in the world and I believe that it comes from judging ourselves. The shift from self-loathing to self-love is the move we all have to make to achieve an awakening. Here's how you can quiet your inner judge courtesy of Transformation Catalyst, Christine Kloser:

Trash Talk/Truth Talk

Step 1: Write down any "trash" voices that you hear in your head. For example: *I'm not good enough, I'm not smart enough*, etc.

Step 2: Take a few deep breaths and connect with that quiet part inside of you that speaks to you with love and compassion.

Step 3: On a separate piece of paper, write down the positive, loving words you hear. For example: *I am a risk taker, I am an inspiration, I am beautiful,* etc.

Step 4: Take the first paper that contained your trash thoughts. Wad it up or tear into little pieces and flush it or burn it. Let go and move on.

The trash we tell ourselves projects out in so many ways. We attract the wrong partners, experience bullying, subject ourselves to negative work situations and carry anger, disappointment and resentment that can translate to fatigue and even illness.

In striving to quiet your inner judge, you'll find a path to acceptance and newfound courage to explore who you really are and what you can bring to the world.

Raising self-esteem starts by listening without prejudice and understanding the difference between judgment and discernment.

How To Let Go Of Blame and Guilt

Business leaders know that they're not perfect and never will be.

I've been thinking about right and wrong, black and white, good and bad and I'm finding less and less use for these definitive terms, especially when it comes to myself. So much of my time has been wasted ruminating over how I just didn't get it right with this client or that employee. My natural tendency is take 100% of the blame for anything that goes *wrong*. I find that's what most people who own service businesses do naturally. It's a heavy load to carry.

To let go of the blame and emerge confidently, I've had to forgive myself and own the idea that maybe others had a hand in causing me pain. Recently, I made an inventory of uncomfortable business moments – the powerful boss who pinned me against my drafting table when I was only 22, the client who threatened to fire me if didn't do more work for free, the disgruntled employee who sent nasty emails, the designer who disappeared in the middle of a job. If you've been working as long as I have, things are bound to happen, not all of them good.

I could tell you that these challenges were life lessons or that we all have a cross to bear or that giants will always block your path on the way to your destiny. But you've heard that stuff before and frankly, when you're falling down the rabbit hole, knowing these truths don't really help. What does stop me from taking a baseball bat to my psyche is stepping back and asking, "Is it really important?" In the grand scheme of things, is this little thing that's turning me inside out worth ruining my health or stressing my family?

What's standing between you and where you want to go could be the disappointment and hurt that lives deep inside of you.

There's no doubt that you've stood on uncertain ground as you've tried to find your footing. Most of us are striving to be good and ethical in a confusing world. You may think that you've done things that are unforgiveable or that others don't deserve your forgiveness. I get it. But what I've found is that resentment just blocks creative energy and keeps you from achieving your dreams.

Last winter I made a commitment to forgive those that I felt had wronged me in work and in life and I put myself at the top of that list. I invite you to do the same and while you're at it, vow to hold yourself accountable, but not see yourself as wrong or bad, just a human being doing the best you can.

The Backlash of Trying To Be Perfect

Any winner knows that making mistakes is part of the game. So why do we keep beating ourselves up?

There is no doubt that rewards can come your way if you exceed expectations. On the other hand, you could experience a definite backlash if you are constantly striving for perfection. First and foremost, it can be debilitating. If you have a perfectionist boss, you know exactly what I mean. No matter how hard you try, you can never do anything 100% right in their eyes. And because they suffer from "analysis paralysis," the entire department lives in Limbo Land. When they fail, they secretly blame it on themselves and turn on you. If you also carry the perfectionist gene, you can easily become their victim and do double duty with your own self-flogging.

As a recovering perfectionist, my natural tendency is to beat myself up when I think I've missed the mark. I don't even need someone to tell me I'm not good enough. I take care of that myself. Like many of us, I was taught to be "good" and I obliged. I felt my father's love fully when his conditions were met and his rules were followed. So I did what was told and learned to feel good about myself when I received a pat on the back – always looking outside myself to cultivate self worth.

Working to do the best you can is one thing; striving for perfection is another.

What I've discovered along the way is that perfectionism can be a principal barrier to success. Although there can be value in it, it's more often another place where we get stuck. If you feel that your career is parked in neutral, maybe it's because perfectionism is your roadblock.

Five Symptoms of Perfectionism

1. Rewriting and rewriting, often becoming less confident with every new version

2. Rethinking, or neatening, or categorizing, or reorganizing

3. Obsessing when someone doesn't seem to approve of you or your work

4. Looking for recognition or reward when you finish a project or task

5. Beating yourself up when you feel you somehow missed the mark

Professionals who have a No-Fear Career keep their eyes on the big picture and don't get caught up in the details. Perfectionism can bog you down in details and can overwhelm objectivity, which can be disastrous in business.

Case in point, I have a client who wants everything she does to be perfect, according to her exceedingly high specifications for perfection. When things don't go exactly as she envisions them, she becomes disappointed in herself. This is true in her cooking, her gardening, her parenting and her work. But how many things ever go just as we picture them? My client's perfectionism keeps her down—and I mean that in two ways: What she counts as her lack of perfection causes her to feel bad about herself, and that lack of self-esteem keeps her from moving ahead.

Even if it were achievable, few of us would get a gold medal at work for our perfectionism. For me, the whole trick to softening or finding balance for my perfectionistic nature is to have a clear vision and mission for my work. It's also about going inside to find happiness, rather than seeking approval and recognition outside. There is little creativity and authenticity in perfectionism. It's only when we stop judging ourselves and others, listen to our gut, act spontaneously, and let our creativity flow that we can demonstrate fearless leadership and be most effective at work.

Going for excellence is worthwhile; trying for perfection is pure ego.

Stopping The Approval-Seeking Cycle

If you're looking for validation from your boss, co-workers or clients – look inside yourself instead.

There's really no substitute for healthy self-esteem, but many of us try to find it outside of ourselves. Instead of doing good work for our own satisfaction, we do it for the approval of others.

If as a child you performed to get positive attention or the love you craved, more than likely your need to take care of everything and everyone – to always be uber-responsible– continues today. The good news is your desire to please may actually be working for you on many levels – over-delivering and overachieving play well in the workplace. Sixty-hour work weeks can often lead to bigger titles and more money. On the flip side, working that hard can also produce stress-related illnesses, divorce and alcoholism.

In his book, "Healing The Shame That Binds You," John Bradshaw talks about high achievers who seek approval from a place of shame. For those of us who played the family hero growing up, we can end up becoming "human doings" instead of human beings: performing to overcompensate for bad feelings about ourselves. That's codependent.

Codependency is defined as "a loss of personal identity in a process of painful external validation." Below are different types of workplace scenarios charged with co-dependency:

Your Boss = Your Parent

Often I see my clients put their bosses in parental roles – seeking their approval and special handouts. If their reaction isn't what they expect, they feel unhappy and unfulfilled.

Your Partner = Your Lover

Not only did I work with my former husband, but I have also consulted with many couples in a struggle for control and power. There's often difficulty recognizing individual needs and wants while each partner tries to convince the other of what they *should* think or feel.

Validation By Client

Many of us in the service business are people pleasers without boundaries looking for recognition and praise. By focusing on meeting our client's needs we are secretly looking to meet our own.

Work Spouse

It can be a positive thing to find a co-worker who will climb the corporate ladder with you. But often these turn into one up/one down relationship where resentments can form easily.

Ask yourself: are you sacrificing yourself to boost your boss, client or co-worker?

If you're in the habit of throwing out a life preserver to those that need to be rescued, I'm guessing that you're exhausted! That's because codependency doesn't work in the long run. You'll eventually hit a wall. To find out if you already have, answer these four questions honestly:

Do I control others to relieve my fears?

Do I let others control me for fear of their abuse or neglect?

Do I adapt or change behavior for others?

Do I validate my value and worth as a person through others?

If you answered "yes" to any of these questions, start to become aware of the underlying feelings you have when you are controlling, caretaking, fixing, rescuing, people pleasing or playing the victim or martyr. You'll begin to realize that you may not be acting out these behaviors from a loving place, but a lonely place. Lao-Tzu, the founder of Taoism once said, "If I keep from imposing on people, they become themselves." It took me a long time to see the truth in this and when I did, it set me and everyone else in my life free.

What can you do today to become interdependent instead of codependent at work?

Making Friends
With Uncertainty

3 steps to having a mission-driven career and the courage to attract greater recognition and more satisfaction.

None of us have a crystal ball that can predict all the chaos that can happen in any given day. In fact, trying to foresee or control the future is pointless. With technology advancing every minute, buying habits changing on a dime, and employers continuing to operate from a place of fear, things have never been more uncertain or challenges greater.

Where we fall short as business leaders is in looking for someone to blame when we feel overwhelmed or undermined by the changes – rather than letting go and surrendering to what's happening – managing the chaos one step at a time with grace, and with faith.

Today we are all being called to move forward in the face of unpredictability and to deal with the here and now. However, not all of us are finding the fortitude to answer the call. Many of us are stuck – longing for a time when things were easier and opportunities just came our way.

To find more satisfaction in your work, you have to accept what is and fearlessly adjust to it.

The next time you are consumed with that aching feeling of failure or you're frozen with fear, try these three steps to gaining greater recognition, higher income and more satisfaction. I call them "The Three A's."

Step One: Accept

Instead of pushing yourself and everyone else up against a wall, tune in to the truth of your situation by making a list of every single thing you must accept that you can't control or change. In my own career I've had to walk away from jobs, clients and business ideas that simply were not working out. Accepting that a certain project or business relationship is going nowhere is progress, not failure.

Step Two: Adjust

Once you accept the truth of your situation, it's time to adjust without blame or judgment. To do so, start by really living in each moment fully – not in the future or the past. Then, get into action by mustering the courage to make big changes.

Why change? Well, according to an Oxford Economics study by Scott Muff of Bellevue

University, to stay competitive in the global marketplace over the next decade, American workers will have to possess four skill sets:

1. **<u>Digital Skills</u>:** The fast-growing digital economy is increasing the demand for highly skilled technical workers.

2. **<u>Agile Thinking</u>:** In a period of sustained uncertainty, where economic, political and market conditions can change suddenly, agile thinking and the ability to prepare for multiple scenarios is vital.

3. **<u>Interpersonal and Communication Skills</u>:** Human resources executives believe that co-creativity and brainstorming skills will be greatly in demand, as will relationship building and teaming skills.

4. **<u>Global Operating Skills</u>:** In a global economy, the ability to manage diverse employees is seen as vastly important over the next five to ten years.

Taking courses to learn one or more of these skills is an adjustment that will be well worth your investment of time and money. If you possess any of these skills now, make sure to shine a light on them wherever your personal brand is seen.

Step Three: Access

Moving through uncertainty and demonstrating that agile thinking that's so prized in the workplace requires stepping out of fear and into faith. When you quiet your mind and access your highest self, you'll find the confidence to do the next right thing. My recommendation is that you don't do it alone. Pull in your biggest supporters and co-create a new vision. When you do, you'll access that part of you that's exceptional, generous, forgiving and truthful.

To have a No-Fear Career, you have to create a clear mission and be able to communicate it to the world while practicing these three steps consistently. In this way, you will make fearlessness a habit— ingrained in every action—so you can change with the times and make them your own.

It's about living big and going deep. We all have unique qualities; it's time to live them in a big way.

Compromise A Little To Keep a Whole Lot

What has digging your heels in ever gotten you? Most likely nothing.

A couple of years ago a friend of mine went to pick up pizza at a local place. When he walked in the restaurant, he immediately spotted some good friends dining with a couple visiting from Texas. They were talking politics when he stopped by their table. The Texas woman asked my friend which candidate he would be voting for in the upcoming election. He said, "President Obama." In response, she called my friend a socialist and a communist and began throwing crusts of pizza at him.

I'm not telling you this story to start a political debate. That's not my intention. What I do want to ask is this: What ever happened to civility and compromise? It seems that everywhere you look, people are becoming more and more judgmental and rigid in their views. Where is it getting us? Nowhere.

Compromise is not about scarcity – it's about abundance. It's defined as the settlement of differences by mutual concessions – *mutual* being the operative word. It may not be human nature to compromise, but it is the path to conflict resolution, and ultimately, peace and prosperity.

Obtaining peace requires us to show up in faith, not fear, and in service of the greater good.

In the work I do with my clients, I advocate for telling the truth and creating consensus. I work with companies to dig deep to uncover the essence of their brands so they can inspire everyone in their organizations to reach their highest potential. During the process, leaders and workers inevitably fall into a fear mode, because what has to be done requires real change.

How do I get my clients out of their own way? By constantly reminding them of the goals they want to achieve, the mission they are on and their core values. To get everyone on the same page requires compromise (and a lot of patience). Ultimately, creating a mutual consensus changes the culture and the way we do business for the better.

Should there be peace at any price? No. That's why it's important to be clear about the line you won't cross.

In business, the challenge when you find middle ground —and the opportunity— is to do so without compromising your core values. That's the distinguishing line. If you compromise your core, you lose yourself. As I've shared with you previously, my core values are love, safety and integrity. What are yours? Being clear will help you make decisions, and trust the decisions you make.

I believe that the lack of civility that exists today stems from fear, which breeds zealous extremists and fundamentalists who ruin it for everyone in the middle. I don't think that a rigid mentality is what's needed in a world in turmoil and so completely divided. Pizza throwing aside, I think it's high time we started listening to each other, embracing our differences and finding common ground.

What can you do today to practice civility, strike a balance with people you are at odds with and create compromise?

Step 3:
Make Your Own Luck

They say the harder you work, the luckier you get. To stand out and attract opportunities, you have to be solidly grounded in who you are—without apology.

In this step you will learn to:

Plot Your Career Destiny

Master The Law of Attraction

Get Clear On Your Goals

Think About Going Back To School

How To Plot A Course To Your Career Destiny

Aim higher with a vision statement that takes you to the nexus of purpose and potential.

"So tell me, where do you see yourself in five years?" I've always had disdain for that frequently asked and totally uninspired interview question. After all, it's not about the next five years – it's about your whole life! The question should be, "What kind of impact do you want to make in the world and how do you want to be recognized for it?"

The only way to give a thoughtful response to that question is to sit down and imagine what you really want for your career and then craft a succinct vision statement that sums up your audacious dream so that it can take flight.

Having a vision statement can give your career a clear picture. It can serve as an inspiration and framework for decision making and planning. The purpose of your vision statement is to stretch boundaries and comfort zones – empowering you to have a sense of what can be.

The vision statement answers the question, "Where do I want to go?" and it delivers a cosmic view of possibilities. It can be uncharted and far-reaching – even farfetched. What it can never be is small minded and laced with fear.

Marianne Williamson once said, "Our deepest fear is not that we are inadequate. Our deepest fear is that we are powerful beyond measure. It is our light, not our darkness that most frightens us. We ask ourselves, 'Who am I to be brilliant, gorgeous, talented, fabulous?' Actually, who are you not to be? You are a child of God. Your playing small does not serve the world."

Articulate your vision statement: crystallize a view of who you can be and what you can do.

The most successful companies in the world write vision statements. When the statement is short and memorable, it can lead the company to do incredible, sometimes unthinkable things. Look at what Microsoft wrote for their vision statement back in the 1980's: "A computer in every home running Microsoft software." This vision statement may have seemed unattainable to most people back then. In fact, I'm sure there were employees inside the company who were afraid of the largesse of the task. Yet it served as a North Star that has driven Microsoft's success to this day.

Whether it's Ford's vision "To become the world's leading Consumer Company for automotive products and services" or Nike's vision "To be the number one athletic company in the world," there's a sense of fearlessness – of destiny – as if planting your flag and liberating yourself is to say, "This is who I am and this is how far I can go."

It's time to look ahead and set an intention – a new vision for your life. Different from your mission, which answers *why* you do what you do, your vision statement sets in motion your career destiny. It should be so big you feel a little scared just writing it down, but do it anyway. Then surround yourself with the right people who will cheer you on as you say "yes" to opportunities that will manifest your vision.

Write a vision statement to achieve your dream and you'll inspire the energy within yourself to get it done.

Mastering The Law of Career Attraction

If everything you're seeking is seeking you, then you better get clear on what you really want.

Every day I meet professionals who feel stuck in their career. Although they've achieved a great deal, they don't know where the road is taking them. Many want to move forward, but the economy and a tough job market have held them in place. It's true that these are real barriers, but I believe that a lack of vision and a clear intention is what's *really* holding them back.

As I've just mentioned, a vision statement serves to guide your career like a North Star. My professional vision statement is *to become the world's most sought after authority on brand creation and reinvention.* Like any powerful vision statement, it reminds me of who I am and where I'm going. When I say, "sought after" I am referring to the idea of being booked solid and not having to constantly pitch or audition for business.

To manifest this vision, I've hired experts – a business coach, social media expert and Internet marketing genius. With their help, I've attracted opportunities from a major movie studio, television network and toy manufacture – all that align with my vision.

This is beyond "The Secret." This is about declaring something audacious and backing it up with a plan.

To get clear on what you really want to happen next in your career and create a plan to get there, take the following steps:

Step 1: Sculpt A Vision For Your Career

Write a crisp vision statement that celebrates your potential. Make sure it inspires you to get out of bed in the morning and do your best.

Step 2: Make A Plan of Action

Figure out the steps you need to take to reach your goals. You may have to learn a new skill, software or language. You'll have to get out and network, blog, tweet or even relocate.

Step 3: Hire Experts To Support Your Vision

Surround yourself with specialists in the areas you'll need to grow into. If you want to be a speaker, hire a speaking coach. If you want to write a book, find a good agent.

Step 4: Stay Open To Opportunity

Once you've set your intention, you'll have to read the signposts along the way to uncover the people and projects that will take you to where you want to go. Watch out for detours.

Step 5: Manifest Your Desires

As you begin your journey, remember these Law of Attraction principles:

- Stay in the positive: your words, your dreams, and your thoughts have power
- Think about your career with faith, hope, love and action
- Don't be afraid to believe you can have what you want and deserve

When I was younger and unaware of these principles, I'd blame everyone and everything for what was going wrong in my career. I'd play victim. Now I look inside. As I become conscious of my own negative thinking, I turn it around by self-talking my way out of the cycle. In no time I'm attracting the right people and circumstances to manifest my vision.

Decide where you want to go and make a road map. Remember, be careful what you ask for— you might just get it!

Get Clear On Your Goals

When you clearly define your goals, you come that much closer to actualizing your dreams.

When you finally uncover and get serious about your heart's desire, the universe starts listening. You may think you've told the universe by saying: "I want a promotion..I want a spouse..I want my own business." I'm telling you that's not enough. You must specifically define your dreams to set them in motion. "I want" doesn't cut it.

Sometime ago, I coached a 40-something woman who wanted to make a move from being a Hollywood producer to a digital content creator. We branded her the "digital storyteller". She started introducing herself that way at networking events, and people started listening. With no online experience, she transferred her movie-making talent to a new medium and very soon scored her dream job! Today she runs a documentary film company that distributes digital content. All by declaring her dream to the world, it came true.

It's the old story: say it and you'll become it, write it down and you'll unleash the power within.

Just like my client, it's critical for you to map out your goals because when you commit your dreams to paper, you release them out into the world. Then when you speak of your dreams, you move them another inch closer to reality.

In order to create a guiding light for your career, type up or write down in your journal the following:

1. State three things you deeply desire
2. Your personal goals for the next 90 days
3. Your professional goals for the next 90 days
4. The impact you want to make on the world
5. How you would like to be recognized

Your goal might be to earn six figures or to get three choice projects handed to you, or be promoted to upper management, or to earn an industry award or receive mention in a trade journal. Or maybe your goal is to be respected by your boss, or to break out altogether by starting your own company or non-profit. Whatever your dream, putting it down on paper is the key to breaking through what's holding you back and unlocking your success.

When you write down your dreams you'll find power in the pen. Your dreams may not have anything to do with your current job or chosen profession. Write them down anyway. What does living well look like, what does it contain? Be very specific and write paragraphs.

Begin by talking about your goals and dreams with people who you know will be supportive. The more you put your dreams out there, the more powerfully they will be brought back to you in reality. Begin today by letting go of any superstition. Tell everyone your wish the next time you blow out your birthday candles. You'll be one step closer to making it come true.

Dreams come true when we take responsibility for the things we want.

Think About Going Back To School

With fewer opportunities for advancement, 60% of Americans are considering going back to school. Should you?

Last week during my monthly touch-up, my hairstylist announced that he was going back to school. George was excited about transferring his talent for making people beautiful into a new career as a plastic surgeon. His plan is to work his way through school over the next seven years. I was completely inspired by George's focused determination to reinvent himself, and I knew that he wasn't alone. Frustrated by dead-end careers, a lack of job prospects and the need to enhance skill sets or be left in the dust, adults are going back to school in droves.

Wanting to find out more about this trend, I asked Jim Maxwell at Bellevue University to share with me the new reality of the adult student. Recently, Bellevue completed a study revealing that adults aged 25 – 54 are struggling the most in this economy. In fact, 23% of working adults are unhappy in their jobs. They report wanting to change the type of work they do in favor of something they actually enjoy. Sound familiar?

Then there are the millions of Americans who are out of work – who have been displaced across industries in decline. If you count yourself among these folks, you need to deal with the changes and take action now, so you can secure a job in an industry that is growing. That action most definitely will involve going back to school.

Here's Jim's advice to adult learners:

1. Don't just get "a degree." Find something that fuels your passion and is relevant to the

market – a degree that employers will respect and value.

2. Look for a program that's flexible so that you can continue to work. That may mean online courses or finding a classroom with adult learners.

3. Make sure that whatever program you get into isn't just about theory, but it gives you a chance to put theory into practice.

4. Find a school that can help you make connections so that you graduate with more than a degree, but real world experience and a job.

I know you'll be tempted to go for an MBA, but before you do, dig deep to find a degree that matches your strengths, not just one that looks good on a resume. You'll also want to explore which degrees will be in demand in 2018 and beyond.

Change is not your enemy; it's your ally. Change is not happening to you, it's happening for you.

Whether you go to grad school or not, you need to be ready, not rusty, for what's next. You could suddenly be let go or made the head of your department. You could land a big contract or be stiffed on a deal. Change is everywhere and you can't predict what's around the corner. That's why it's so important to keep learning. Becoming stale, complacent, stagnant—these options are unworthy of you.

To embrace change, sharpen your saw by taking marketing, sales, leadership, public speaking or computer courses after work. Make connections through volunteering, joining a team sport, attending conferences or teaching a class. Or, like my hairstylist and over half of American workers today, go back to school and stretch yourself to earn a desirable degree.

It's time to think of the actions you can take to reach your next peak and resist that doubting voice. When you stop being afraid of change, and you get in step with the ever-changing business environment, the landscape of what's foreign to you shrinks—and so does the distance between you, others and your career destiny.

Stay open. Until you take your last breath, don't let learning end until your life does.

Step 4:
Become A Rainmaker

So many professionals I know have a tendency to hide behind email. If you're guilty of this, then it's time to go to a networking event or attend a conference and connect with prospective partners, clients and employers. This step will help you confidently tell them why you'll be an asset to their business. Remember, you've got to get out to get in!

In this step you will learn to:

Become a Closer

Change Your Approach

Show Up When You Want To Give Up

Create a Memorable Tagline

Discovery Your Worth

Know Your Audience

Befriend the Top Brass

Find the Right Partner

Be a Great Client

How To Sell Your Ideas Like Don Draper

Could playing small be what's keeping you from winning big in business?

Each time I sit down to watch an episode of *Mad Men* I'm drawn in by the power that Don Draper commands in a meeting. He knows that he's got the right idea. His cocksure pitch blankets the client in confidence. With total faith, they believe that the campaign will work to increase sales and build their personal reputations as genius decision makers. And whether it's Cool Whip or Clearasil, Don and the *Mad Men* of Sterling Cooper Draper Pryce deliver.

What keeps many talented professionals from selling their ideas or closing a deal? In a word: fear. Afraid of rejection or being seen as out of touch, or worse stupid, they present with apology and have a compromised strategy in their back pocket should their original thinking be shot down in flames.

Getting your idea rejected is not the end of the road–it's a speed bump.

My personal struggle in developing that Don Draper-like swagger came from not really understanding or owning my personal power. I'd give it away by trying to please everyone. My motivation? I wanted to be liked... desperately. I would take on every job, even when I was stretched. I'd have a terrible time saying "no" when I should have.

This fear-based "dancing bear" behavior came to an end at a meeting with the president of a top financial company. After I had created the firm's brand strategy, I was asked to conceive a new advertising campaign. During the pitch, I showed my client three different directions and then quietly asked, "Which one do you like best?" He suddenly got red in the face, rose from his chair and pounded the desk with his fist and said, "I pay you a lot of money to help me build this brand. Now stop trying to please me and YOU TELL ME which campaign to run!" That meeting was a wake up call to peel the dancing bear mask right off. I did it little by little everyday with practice, because I knew that dancing bear behavior didn't resonate with my soul or serve my personal brand.

Don Draper is no dancing bear. He doesn't second-guess how the client may react to what he's presenting or try to adjust to a mediocre mindset. Rather, he confidently steps up to the plate, grasps the bat of clarity firmly, and calmly sets his sights. Then he swings for the fences. If he strikes out he knows there will be other times up at bat. And heck, if they don't get what he's pitching, to hell with them—there are other clients out there that will.

When it's time for you to get in the big idea game, be mindful of your expectations. People will be people, and each one will have their individual responses. After all, judgment is the social currency of our society. Pitch and then detach so you can easily roll with the punches. The more you're invested in a specific outcome, the greater your disappointment if things don't go as you imagined.

The big lesson here is to say what you need to say in a way that benefits your company or client. Make sure that you honor the company's mission and the people receiving your ideas. If you are confident and enthusiastic about your concept, you'll be seen as a fearless leader who can make a positive impact.

A special note for those that take pitches and hire outside creative partners and consultants: if you have the attitude that these folks are lucky to be working for you or they should be kowtowing to your every whim, now is the time to change your thinking. Why? For two reasons: 1) they are your link to the outside world and, 2) they could be your ticket to stardom. If you put your faith in their talents the way that Don Draper's clients do, you'll reap rewards. On the flip side, if you try to control, diminish or intimidate them, you could tarnish your reputation and sabotage results.

As Don Draper boldly said in Season 4 of Mad Men, "You want some respect? Go out and get it for yourself."

How To Get to "Yes" When Everyone is Saying "No"

Take a look at these sure fire strategies from master closers that will help you attract opportunities and more business.

My father is a hero, not just because he was a Marine in WWII who fought bravely in the Pacific, but because when he got stateside, he became a world-class advertising sales guy, a real closer. To this day, he regales me with *Mad Men*-style stories about his time at Los Angeles' KABC radio in the '60s. Can you say stewardesses, martinis and Playboy Bunnies?

My dad still tells me, "You've got to over-deliver, baby! That's how you get the business and keep them coming back." He also taught me that enthusiasm was the secret sauce to any successful salesperson. Needless to say I'm one over-delivering, enthusiastic closer. I thought I had learned everything I needed to know about closing from my dear old dad until Superstar Sales Coach Linda Clemons threw her sales mojo at our Big Fish Mastermind Group during our monthly call. Holy cow can that woman deliver numbers!

Before you try to sell your product or service, find out your prospect's pain points.

I've been saying for the past few years that no one should be selling, they should be *serving*. Linda echoed this and instructed us to ask our potential clients, "What is keeping you up at night?" Or, "Are you happy with where you are at right now?"

She told us that our job was to relieve our client's pain and enhance their pleasure. She said, "Your service should answer your prospect's needs and wants. You have to find out what's important to them and link that to your product."

What if they think that what you're offering is too expensive? If you build a powerful value proposition you can overcome most objections.

In a tough economy it's not uncommon to be challenged on pricing. Linda has some great comebacks when your prospect says, "You're too expensive." Here are my two favorites:

"As compared to what?"

"Apparently you have a reason for feeling that way, may I ask you what it is?"

Sometimes it's not about price at all. Your prospect seems elusive and they are down right playing hard to get. What do you do? Well, for starters, know that they would be running away if they didn't want to be caught. You have to sell them more! "It's KNOW, not NO," Linda says.

One of the worst things you can do when you are pitching a prospect is talk too much and oversell. But, how do you know when to shut up? My dad always said to give great eye contact and listen carefully. If you are present, your prospect will let you know when you've lost them. Linda adds to this wisdom with three powerful slogans:

1) When in doubt, leave it out.
2) When you go long, you go wrong.
3) If you confuse them, you'll lose them.

In other words, tell your story lickety-split – making your prospect the main character. Keep your on-screen presentation crisp and visually exciting. Delete anything resembling an eye chart or teleprompter. And if the vibe is right, bring on the martinis old school style!

Become a closer today by serving, not selling. You'll get to "Yes" a whole lot faster!

Showing Up When You Want To Give Up

You are your word. Here's how to stay in integrity when you've had enough.

The week before Christmas I had a big workday planned in Los Angeles with clients at Sony Pictures Television and FOX. Rather than fly in the night before and miss dinner with my daughter, I decided to take the 7:30am flight out of Albuquerque.

I got up at 3:30am, did my make-up and hair and slipped on a dark grey sleeveless Jackie-O style dress, a pair of Trina Turk high black boots and a leopard print trench. I was dressed for a winter's day in LA, not Santa Fe where it was freezing cold with snow and ice on the ground.

At 4:30am my cab driver called from the gate. I pressed a key to let him in and waited at the door with my suitcase and computer bag. Ten minutes passed and the phone rang again. The cab had slid down the steep gravel road to my home. The driver told me I'd have to walk to the gate to meet him. I grabbed a pair of gloves, scarf and flashlight and slogged through the snow, wheeling my suitcase behind me.

After a long walk to the top of the hill, I could see the driver's headlights below shinning through the gate. I became overwhelmed with the situation and longed to sit down in the snow and just give up.

Separated from my husband, the feelings of loss for our 16-year relationship flooded through me. I was now a single working mom, and in that moment, I realized that I was really on my own and no one was coming to save me. The headlights almost blinded me as the driver shouted, "YOU CAN DO IT!" I planted my boots carefully in the snow to avoid the ice and slowly made it down the treacherous hill through the gate and into the cab.

When you feel your confidence slipping, resist the urge to give up and courageously show up.

Two weeks earlier, my client from Food Network called to ask if I would get on a plane that day to fly to New York. A nor'easter was coming. It was likely my scheduled flight would be cancelled the next day, so if I didn't leave immediately I could leave a room full of executives in a lurch. I dropped my daughter at a friend's house and found a flight out before the storm hit.

Woody Allen once said that 80% of success is showing up. In the dead of winter, in the cold black night, the path to your destiny can be covered in snow and ice—making you feel lost and alone. It's only when you break through your fear and take one step forward, and then another, that you show up as a leader, a solid partner and someone in service to others.

I learned long ago that *you are your word.* You can't underestimate the power of being someone who shows up consistently. I added a major client last year because a competitor didn't follow through. Over the last two decades, I've won a staggering number of projects, not necessarily because I was the client's first choice, but because another vendor dropped the ball while I stayed in the game.

During that pre-Christmas trip to LA I would have never imagined that my taxi wouldn't be able to make it up my drive or that a monumental snowstorm would hit New York a few days after Halloween. None of us have a crystal ball that can predict all the challenges that can arise in any given day in our personal lives or at work. In fact, trying to foresee or control the future is pointless.

In this Age of Transparency, success comes to those who are a sure bet. Believe in yourself and resist the temptation to feel entitled, play victim or put roadblocks in the way of what needs to be done. I think you'll find that letting go of fear and stepping into faith is the answer.

Never underestimate the power of being someone others can count on.

Change Your Approach

Quality and customer service are no longer differentiators. Innovation is what creates a sustainable competitive advantage.

What's driving success today in large corporations and small businesses is not traditional marketing; it's innovation. Quality and customer service are no longer differentiators. Innovation is what creates a sustainable competitive advantage.

So basically, everything we know about marketing is dead wrong. It's not about PUSHING a product or service (the very definition of marketing); it's about PULLING the customer in with great ideas that penetrate hearts and minds.

Courageous leaders are changing their approach from one that is sales-driven to one that creates an emotional connection and builds relationships. To fearlessly alter the way you are going after opportunities, engage your key employees and partners in writing an inspiring mission, vision and set of values. Enriching and unifying, these guidelines will motivate you and everyone you work with to radiate out love for your company's service and products.

Courageous leaders galvanize their workforce with a clear mission, vision and set of values.

Crafting these guidelines as a team is more valuable than ever because we work in an interconnected and interdependent world where everyone wants to feel empowered. Yet, organizations are still structured in silos and dictate top down. A culture of innovation based on common purpose breaks down these barriers.

Having an impassioned sales force that shines out to customers cannot be achieved simply by rallying the troops at an off-site with team building exercises and excessive drinking. There must be a brand centric focus year round – one that's holistically built from the inside out. Only then can a substantive relationship exist between company and customer.

What I've learned as an executive at Turner Broadcasting and as a brand strategist to the world's largest entertainment companies is that people need a North Star to guide them to do great work.

When encouraged to creatively meet customer demand, employees tend to invent new ideas and products that can change the world for the better.

Rather than being PUSHED to buy, customers are PULLED in by the company's value, which is reflected in attitude and in every action.

Forget the notion of marketing. Create a culture of fearless innovation and your business will thrive for years to come.

3 Steps To Creating A Memorable Tagline

Take charge! Transcend the title your company gave you and define yourself.

If you're having trouble describing yourself quickly and with punch, here is the solution: create a tagline. A tagline speaks volumes about who you are and what you can do in a short phrase. If conceived correctly, your tagline will make an unforgettable impression.

Rather than introducing myself as CEO of Big Fish Marketing, which lacks any interest or emotional connection, I say, "I'm Robin Fisher Roffer... I reinvent brands and reignite professionals." My tagline gives me an immediate positive reaction and invites conversation.

That line goes on the home page of my website, my Facebook profile and LinkedIn page. I also use it to sign off my emails. This lets my target audience knows what I can do for them without taking the 30-second ride up the preverbal elevator.

Just do it! Make your personal tagline a succinct expression that differentiates you from the pack. Here are 3 powerful steps to creating your tagline:

Step 1: Identify your unique skills and best qualities, and create a list of descriptive words and phrases that correspond to your professional self. Look for something you can deliver that few can and that you love to do.

Step 2: Edit your definition down to a zippy phrase that aligns with your job or the most magnetic aspects of your career. Your tagline should be the verbal equivalent of a logo that will come to people's mind when they hear your name.

Step 3: Make your tagline benefit-driven, aspirational, descriptive or a call to action. "You're in good hands with Allstate" is benefit driven. BMW's tagline is descriptive, "The Ultimate Driving Machine," Nike's "Just Do It" is aspirational, while American Express' tagline "Take Charge," is a call to action.

The personal tagline you use to define and position yourself should be simple, positive and unique. A clear, concise declaration of what you do, what makes you special, and why the world should care, your tagline should be short (6 words or less) and not too cute or clever.

I have a friend who's an "Eco-Journalist," another who's a "Book Doctor," and one who calls herself "The Transformation Catalyst." I recently worked with Greg Clark at Hallmark Channel on his tagline and we came up with "Marketing Specialist. Ratings Driver." A computer consultant I know who not only fixes IT problems, but also calms down stressed out, tech-challenged executives, uses the tagline "Cyber Therapist."

So aren't you more than an Office Assistant, Director of Marketing, Account Executive or VP of Finance? Sure you are! Create a tagline that frames you as relevant and valuable. Make your tagline descriptive, aspirational, benefit driven or a call to action. Don't allow the world to define you. The next time you go to a networking event, honor your talents by revealing your dynamic spirit in a captivating tagline that speaks volumes about you.

Think different! Make your tagline express that incredible mix of everything that makes you undeniably unique and valuable.

What Are You Really Worth?

Pricing yourself can be tough. Here's five ways to determine if you're in the ballpark.

For most of my life I've had personal issues around money. That's because during my childhood I lived for many years in impoverished circumstances. It made me absolutely sure I never wanted to go there again. In a way it gave me my first life goal: to never be poor, to always have enough—to have more than enough—to keep a reserve, a safety net.

Although I've had my own business for more than two decades, there isn't a day that goes by that I don't wrestle with what to charge clients for my services. On the one hand, I have no problem asking for a big number. On the other hand, as soon as I hit "send" and that contract goes out, I churn with uncertainty. Did I charge too much or too little? In this economy, you can never be sure.

My prices are based on four things: 1) the scope of the project, 2) my experience, 3) track record of success and 4) what the competition is charging. When major brands price their products they survey all the other products in their brand's category. Then they position themselves in relation to those other products. Some brands price themselves lower than the competition to attract a bigger customer base – others make themselves very expensive and are promoted as best in class.

Building your value has a lot to do with how you see yourself and how you price yourself.

Much of the cache of driving a Mercedes Benz has to do with its high price. Not just anyone can afford one. That's part of its brand appeal. Customers believe they're getting the best when they pay the most, and the same may be true for you. But, you'd better deliver. Don't pretend to be the best in your field unless you're sure you are. Don't charge more for your services or ask for a salary in excess of industry averages unless you offer "value added" benefits, more than the standard, and can demonstrate it by being consistently more competent, more reliable, more flexible, and quicker—whatever you claim to be.

Here are five ways to determine what you're worth and price yourself accordingly:

1. Figure out what you should be making for someone in your position using a salary calculator.
2. Do additional research by networking with headhunters who can tell you what the going rate is for similar positions over at the competition.
3. Determine your unique value by calculating how much revenue you've generated and/or the elite skills you possess that make you an expert in your field.
4. Meet with a business coach in your industry and ask them to help you position yourself to get the salary you deserve.
5. Go for it and ask for what you really want. If you don't ask, the answer will always be "No."

There have been times when I've felt insecure about my worth and have priced myself too low. A dip in business or a difficult client knocked me off my game and in response I gave myself away. Do yourself a favor and set your price based on real facts and not your emotions.

Except at the very beginning of your career when you might take an unpaid internship, lower salary or fee structure in order to get in the door, don't charge less for your work than you're worth.

And except for extraordinary circumstances, which you'll have to judge for yourself—<u>never</u> give your services away. It's a psychological truth that the recipient will not value work they get for free.

So trade your services, or arrange a payment plan, or extend credit, or agree to a low starting salary with an automatic raise after three months, but don't do it for nothing. You'll never do yourself a favor by putting your brand value at zero.

Keep in mind that we accept the money we think we deserve. Make sure you feel outstanding about you going into any negotiation.

For God's Sake, Don't Be Boring!

Creating an engaging personal brand starts with knowing your audience and showing interest in them.

One night, while attending a small dinner party, my eyes started to glaze over while listening to one of the guests. I said to myself, "This person is so boring." Because I was raised in the Midwest and lived in the South for ten years, I couldn't bring myself to walk away or interrupt (which would have been the only way to stop their incessant self-centered chatter). This person was such a complete narcissist in desperate need of attention that I began to feel like I was doing community service.

With the world the way it is, we all have so little time. Being with someone who clearly has his or her own agenda and never asks you a question or sparks a new idea can be the ultimate time waster. To make the best of any encounter, you have to become the catalyst for conversation that is engaging, real and thoughtful. That can only happen when you ask great questions that reveal insight and interest. By consciously communicating, you make yourself unforgettable and create an emotional connection.

To build meaningful connections, you have to show up with authentic intention.

No matter what your mission or your financial goal or your personal dreams, identifying and earning the devotion of your key influencers is the interlocking and necessary means to reaching those objectives. Who are the key influencers in your life? It's your boss, co-workers, clients, customers – anyone who can make or break your career. To get their attention and make a positive, lasting impression, you've got to know what makes them tick. So before you start talking, you have to get the answers to these burning questions:

Who is my audience?

What is their perception of me?

What do they currently think about my offer?

What do I want them to think?

What motivates them?

How will I attract them to my product/services/company?

How can I create an emotional connection?

Who else is competing for their loyalty?

As the English novelist C.P. Snow once said, "Never overestimate your audience's knowledge, never underestimate their intelligence!" The more you know about your audience and what they need, the more comfortable you're going to feel, and the more meaningful connection you'll be able to make. Once you've established who they are, you have to always be asking yourself these questions:

Do others see me as an authority in my field?

Do they feel I add value to their business?

Do I present a clear solution to their problem?

Have I lost any customers/clients lately?

Do my key influencers seem happy to see me or hear from me?

Have I been passed over for a promotion or a plum project lately?

Has my staff been cut?

Answering these questions honestly will help you to stay relevant to your audience and keep you from appearing stale and boring. It's not all *me, me, me* that gets the deal done. That's a turn off. The key is to make your target audience the main character of your story by answering the question that's on their mind and that is, "What's in it for me if I work with you?"

I used to say, "sell them once and then never stop selling," which is still true. However, marketing today is all about serving people. So the approach that works best now is asking smart questions and then finding ways to tailor your message and personalize it so that it is received as a gift to your client or prospect, and not a mandate. With this in mind, you'll never be seen as boring again.

If you want to create a captivating executive image, do a 180-degree turn and stand in the shoes of the people you need to influence most.

How To Befriend The Top Brass

If you want your personal brand to shine with decision makers, become a fan of their business.

Years ago, when I was an executive at Turner Broadcasting, I would have lunch with the heads of each network on a monthly basis. Although they were presidents and I was just a director, they were interested in how I was leveraging the local power of our affiliates and distributors to increase ratings.

The lunches were productive, fun and lively, something to look forward to. I gained insight on what was important to them and supported their goals with my marketing programs.

At one lunch, I asked CNN's president, "what do you think your audience isn't 'getting' about your network that they should know?" He answered, "That we break news first." From there, I came up with a strategy to send 30-second "CNN Hot Spots" overnight to affiliates when the network was first to cover a big story.

Today, I zero in on what is uniquely important to my clients. During a recent branding workshop with a biomedical company, I asked the owner, "What aren't doctors understanding about your products?" Questions like this are what your clients and/or bosses want to hear. It means you're taking a keen interest in their agenda, product, and future.

Championing the vision of company leaders builds your executive presence and value.

Many roads lead to the top. Befriending the head of the company or department and becoming a fan of his or her vision is the quickest route. It's not about brown nosing or trying to be the teacher's pet. It's about being seen as integral to the company and its success.

Step One: Find Common Interests

To make a real connection, you first have to tune in to what interests the top decision-maker at the place you're working or business you are serving.

Step Two: Get Involved. Be Useful.

Take a 180-degree turn and stand in their shoes. What are his or her pet projects? What does he or she really want? What can you do to help?

Step Three: Demonstrate Enthusiasm

Focused interest and enthusiasm works to create an unbreakable bond between you and the person who can most influence where you go in the company.

Step Four: Sell Your Ideas

"When presenting ideas to decision makers, realize that it is your responsibility to sell, not their responsibility to buy," says Marshall Goldsmith.

Step Five: Focus On Making A Difference

Always look to the greater good as a guide, not your own personal agenda. Don't try to "win" or "be right." Your suggestions should help the overall health of the organization.

When you show genuine interest, your positive energy radiates outward and engages others.

As a brand strategist, I often start my client relationship at the top of the company, but over time I work with marketing and sales executives to execute the strategy. To continue to receive direction from the top, I schedule meetings with their bosses around lunch, drinks, or dinner, and on a social, friendly basis ask about their goals and how things are going. I can then translate that intelligence into smart ideas that make my clients look like stars.

You may be shaking your head thinking that you could never get or don't even deserve a seat at the table. If so, it's critical to believe in yourself and to know that your contributions are valuable. Cultivating this kind of confidence from deep inside of you will spur you forward.

Showing that you are a fan means becoming your own fan first. It requires that you stay positive, find solutions, dedicate yourself to the end game, and not give up when things get tough. Celebrate all the victories (big and small) and you'll find your inner fan to cheerlead your own success and the success of those around you.

Become your own fan and it will become easier to cheerlead those at the top.

Finding The Right Partner

When it comes to business or love, you have to set your intention and make a plan.

Post-divorce I have a lot to be thankful for—a beautiful house in Santa Fe, a smart and engaging teenage daughter, a purpose-driven business and a rich social life. With so much to share, I decided to sit down and write a partnership strategy for me, rather than leave love completely to chance and attract Mr. Wrong.

Consciously seeking a strong partnership— rather than letting it all go to chance isn't just smart— it's good business!

I'd changed so much since the last time I was single. At the mid-point of my life, my wants and needs were completely different than in the past. So when I wrote down my heart's desire…POW…everything clicked! Here are my secrets to finding a partner in love or in business:

SECRET #1: Get Clear On What You Bring To The Table

Write down your strengths, talents, passions and interests to unearth the essence of who you are and what you bring to a relationship. Draw parallels between past partners and try to assess what went wrong and what went right. From this new awareness, you may need to vow to do things differently the next time.

SECRET #2: Imagine Your Life With The Right Partner

Throw out the rulebook. Forget about following your feelings (they usually get you into trouble.) Sit down and write out what your life or your business would be like with the right partner in it. Imagine every aspect of the relationship and what it would bring. Know that being rescued is out of the question and that rescuing someone else will never work. This has to be a win-win deal.

SECRET #3: Define The Qualities You Are Looking For

An "is/is not list" creates a filter for your search. Here's an example of one I would use to find a business partner. Create your own to help you powerfully set your intention (and your boundaries).

My ideal partner is...	My ideal partner is not...
Experienced	Complacent
Confident	Arrogant
Self Sufficient	Needy
Financially Solvent	Desperate
Conscientious	Sloppy
Ambitious	Lazy
Charismatic	Egotistical
Cooperative	Argumentative
Authentic	Faking It
Giving	Co-dependent
Smart	Know-It-All
Open	Stubborn

SECRET #4: Figure Out What's Stopping You

Lots of things can stand in the way of your success. Fear and lack of self-esteem are the big ones. Once you get clear on what's keeping you from attracting the right partner, do what's necessary to instill confidence and courage.

SECRET #5: Spread The Word & Make A Plan

The fastest way to find the right partner is to tell everyone you know what you are looking for and how you plan to complement each other. Then, do research to find the places and events where you could meet your partner – look for workshops, classes, trade association events, online groups, etc. Take out your calendar and fill it up!

SECRET #6: Be Yourself And Tell Your Greatest Story

Once trust is established, tell your story truthfully and in the most positive way without apologizing for yourself. It won't take long for you to become an unforgettable and desirable partner.

If you stand still, you can never move forward. What will you do today to find the partner you've been looking for?

5 Ways To Be A Great Client And Get The Best Work

How to turn your outside partners into your personal brand builders

As an executive at Turner Broadcasting I had the power to hire and fire agencies and consultants. I would hammer them on cost and then swell up with pride. It was a game to me and I felt like the better I played it, the more I'd be valued. That was the lie I told myself. In reality, they were doing great work for me and in turn I was discounting them.

If you have the attitude that your vendors are lucky to be working for you or they should be kowtowing to your every whim, now is the time to change your ways. Why? For two reasons: 1) they are your link to the outside world, and 2) they could be your ticket to stardom.

There's an old adage in the agency business: "You're only as good as your client." Be a good client and you'll get great work that builds your reputation.

Here are five things you can do right now to get the best out of your creative partners courtesy of Rick Heffner, owner of Fuszion Design.

1) **Write A Solid Brief**
   Make sure it contains a project description, objectives, target audience, unique selling proposition, key benefits of your product/service, support of claims, look and feel, brand personality and a realistic budget and timeline.

2) **Search For The Right Partner**
   Don't hire someone because they'll give you a deal. Conduct a proper search and make sure that the outside partner that you choose is well suited for the project and that your work styles are a good match.

3) <u>**Stick To The Timeline**</u>
If your vendor doesn't have all the necessary assets (logos, photos, charts, graphs, copy, etc.) they can't possibly begin your project or meet your deadlines. It's like cooking Chinese food—you have to prep everything before you put the fire under the pot.

4) <u>**Don't Over-Analyze, Go With Your Gut**</u>
Your mother-in-law is not your art director. If you get too many people involved in decision-making, you'll likely end up with something unremarkable. Great ideas don't come from a hodgepodge of opinions – they come from instincts and insights.

5) <u>**Communicate Disappointments Respectfully**</u>
If something doesn't go well, don't be passive/aggressive. Instead, pick up the phone and communicate how you feel using the "sandwich method." First say something complementary, then sandwich in your criticism, then say something positive again. Like a sandwich, it leaves people with a much better taste in their mouth.

Don't try to control or intimidate outside partners. You'll tarnish your reputation and never get the results you want.

Some time ago one of my clients called me to haggle over a small charge. Our contract clearly stated that he owed me the money, but he wanted to dispute it nonetheless. He claimed it would make him *feel better* if he could shave off the overtime. I told him that it was his call. One week later he paid my bill minus the charge. I wonder if he thought he won that round or if his boss patted him on the back for saving the company a few bucks. Either way, he lost all credibility with me.

Make a vow not to play small with your agencies, vendors and consultants. One day you may need them for a recommendation, and reputations tend to linger.

Step 5:
Declare Your Specialty

One important aspect of having a No-Fear Career is to zero in on your specialty and carve out a niche that attracts opportunities and higher fees. Taking this step will help you turn your *skills* into your *area of expertise.*

In this step you will learn to:

Stand Out From The Crowd

Discover your Essence

Recognize your Talents

Take Off the Mask

Declare What Business You're In

Shine a Light on your Differences

Stand Out From The Crowd

Clearly define your expertise so you can attract the opportunities you want and the money you need.

The process of developing a dynamic professional image asks you to unearth your authentic self, identify what you bring to the table, declare your values, envision your future, and at times, live a double life as you evolve into the professional you aspire to be.

The linchpin to distinguishing yourself in business is to declare your area of expertise. What you call your specialty is of major importance to your success in the workplace. The specialist always makes more money than the general practitioner—it almost doesn't matter what the specialty is—as long as its something that sets you apart and is prized by your clients and/or higher-ups.

Magazines are all about specializing. There's Food and Wine, Vogue, Cowboys & Indians, Car & Driver, Architectural Digest, Rolling Stone and Cigar Aficionado. On television there are shopping channels, religious channels, women's channels, sports channels, and channels for kids only, like Nick.

It's the same in my "category". There are many people claiming to be brand strategists, but by specializing in entertainment, I've created a niche that's attracted top clients and commanded substantial fees for over 20 years.

If you're thinking that narrowing your skills could shrink your market or diminish your value, consider this: By choosing entertainment as my area of expertise, I've attracted cosmetics companies, fashion houses and even insurance companies and banks who want to apply the principles of building an audience as we do in entertainment to their own brands. Being a specialist can actually expand your market and turn you into the go-to expert—making you essential and irreplaceable.

If you want to increase job security, specialize. Being a generalist is very old news.

Doctors specialize as oncologists, pediatricians, and psychiatrists. Lawyers come in a variety of flavors: personal injury, criminal, patent, corporate. Teachers specialize by subject and grade. Someone who has spent years gardening has probably also developed specialized knowledge, maybe about growing organic vegetables, designing colorful pots, or pruning trees; and so has someone who has practiced a sport, or mastered a game, or read extensively on any particular subject.

For one of my clients, zeroing in on a specialty was difficult because her talents qualified her in many different areas. She'd studied folk art and design in college. But her parents pushed her to major in communications. At Parsons, she'd fallen in love with the possibilities the Internet held for artists. She saw web design as the folk art of the 21st Century. By building websites for galleries and museums, she could be expansive in a specialized area. Today she has become a star in a galaxy of her own construction.

Your area of expertise—your specialty—doesn't have to be an art or science. You might be someone who develops a reputation as a skilled listener. You might be an expert at relationship building; or a screenwriter specializing in romantic comedy or science fiction; or you could be someone specializing in online consumer research.

It's time to clarify your specialty to ensure your success in this challenging economy. To begin, take out a pad and pen and follow these four powerful steps.

Step 1: Recall What You Have Been Praised For

In order to reveal your true value and potential in business and life, you need to consider what makes you unique. Spend a moment pondering how you have been praised. Think of the praise your parents; friends, teachers, bosses and colleagues have given you. List five common praises you have received.

Step 2: Identify Your Talents and Strengths

What do you do really well? Some examples of personal attributes prized in the workplace include being a team player, reliable and tech savvy, a relationship builder, a dealmaker. Using this list to stimulate your ideas, list five words that describe your strengths and talents.

Step 3: Think About How You Want To Be Known

Out of the five key talents and strengths you listed, which one would you like to develop as a specialty and why? Or is there something else? Make sure that the specialty you chose sets you apart from the pack and is something that is absolutely needed now.

Step 4: Write Your Specialty Statement

What's your specialty and what is its primary benefit to others? For example: "I want to be known as a creative problem solver whose ideas propel our company's business forward."

Research, study and develop your specialty and then declare yourself an expert in your niche. The more you define yourself as the specialist in your category, the more others will perceive you that way and the more money you'll earn.

From the values and talents you possess that have money-making potential, narrow your focus to an area that you can develop as your niche or specialty that aligns with your vision statement. In no time your professional image will become strongly defined and you'll be sought after for your expertise.

Think about what you want to be known for. The more you define yourself, the more well known you'll become and the more money you'll earn.

Discover Your Essence

Owning your true essence and letting go of defense mechanisms is the key to moving forward fearlessly in the world.

In my continuing search to discover my highest self to enjoy a No-Fear Career, I worked with Hans Phillips, a deeply gifted Ontologist from Northern

California. He has developed a methodology that reveals your essence and a practice that empowers you to show up in that shining way consistently.

To begin, Hans asked me to call 10 people in my sphere of influence and ask them to tell me "What shows up when I do? What qualities do I bring into a room?" The fun part was, those that responded could only say nice things about me. After I finished the calls, Hans boiled down the comments into six essence words, which for me were:

Sparkle

Possibility

Enthusiasm

Connection

Power

Grace

Once my essence was revealed, he made me look at my defense mechanisms – those ways of reacting negatively when I'm triggered by uncomfortable situations. I clearly saw through working with Hans that from time to time my dark side (read: fear) would manifest into:

Victim

Martyr

Whiner

Workaholic

Picky

Knowing that I have these dark tendencies and seeing them as fear-based has really helped me to show up in my essence. That's because I want to present myself in my true essence so that I ignite action and my effect on others will be indelible.

So now before I give a speech, show up at a client's office or sit down to write my blog, I say my essence words to myself so that the world can see the real me.

To have a No-Fear Career, keep defense mechanisms at bay and work in your essence.

What Do You Bring To The Table?

To propel your career forward, it's essential to recognize your talents and distinguishing features.

My talents are all about performing: singing, dancing, acting, and public speaking. I have a friend who's a talented pianist and one who's a wonderful painter. I know a woman who can walk into a room where everybody is cranky and at odds, and leave it with everybody smiling and hugs all around. I don't know how she does it, but it's her talent.

By the time we're adults, most of us know a few things we do well. But we may be overlooking talents that have fallen by the wayside. Think back to when you were a kid. What did your parents or teachers praise you for? What were your favorite subjects in school? What extracurricular activities did you like best after school?

For many of us, evolving our natural talents ended with childhood— and so did the monitoring and feedback of parents and teachers. That's why it's extremely important to establish a kind of focus group consisting of your most trusted friends or family members. Think of them as your board of advisors. The companies I work with use focus groups all the time to find out how the public perceives their brands. Because these are your friends and they know you and where you're coming from, you can expect relevant feedback. Ask them to tell you what each of them thinks is your foremost talent. Then write down what they tell you.

This is valuable information, which usually reveals something deeper than the skills you may already be aware of. **THIS INFORMATION COULD BE MORE VALUABLE TO YOUR SUCCESS THAN AN MBA.** Next, ask your focus group to list work-related attributes that apply to you such as accountability, assertiveness, creativity, responsiveness, wisdom, decisiveness and initiative.

Business is a talent show – so don't squander or hide your key attributes – focus on them!

In business, these attributes are as much an expression of talent as an ability to play the violin. They are distinguishing characteristics prized by employers, potential clients and the public in general, no matter what the field.

If you're a "natural" in several areas you might not even be aware you are distinguished by these attributes. That's where the focus group comes in.

You might not consider yourself especially dedicated, but then come to find out that people think your dedication to a project is above and beyond anybody else's. If you adjust easily to a change in circumstances, say a merger or a new boss, you'd be selling yourself short to think you're not any more flexible than the next guy.

Using the list from your focus group to prompt you, adding those words that speak of your unique qualities—your values, your passions, your special skills—make a record of five key attributes that you want to accentuate to key influencers—whether those people are your boss or your colleagues at work, or a prospective employer, or your own clients.

Once you've got your list of five key attributes, write a benefit driven statement for each attribute that will resonate with your target. For example, I could make the claim that I'm an effective communicator. To make that a real benefit, I would say to my clients, "What I bring to the table is effective communication. Not only do I write powerful messages, I can motivate everyone in your organization to consistently use those messages inside your company and out in the world." I would then give an example or case study backing up my claim. This is the process to determine your distinguishing value and the benefits of working with you. Once you have five attributes defined and powerful benefit statements polished, you will be unstoppable!

How can you fearlessly bring your talents and distinguishing features to the table to enhance perception and grow your career?

Can We Just Be Real In Business?

When Creating A Personal Brand, Puffery & Lies Can Only Take You So Far

What trumps a tornado ripping through the South? You got it, "The Donald". Only Donald Trump, the P.T. Barnum of our time, would have the audacity to fly in on his own branded helicopter to hold a press conference in the midst of a disaster to congratulate himself on getting President Obama to turn over his long form birth certificate.

During the 2012 Presidential Campaign, Trump also blasted that our trade with China isn't fair and that american workers are losing jobs to the Chinese. As true as that may be, Trump was out of integrity licensing his name to manufactures who make his branded products in China.

Despite the hair, as a brand strategist, I used to think this guy was a brilliant self-marketer. But, not anymore.

To gain trust and honestly deepen your relationship with those you need to influence the most, (which in Trump's case was the entire US voting population and TV viewers), you have to practice what I call the *Holy Trinity of Branding*: Consistency, Clarity and Authenticity.

Consistency makes you look like a leader. This is about staying on message – synchronizing agreement and action— walking the walk and talking the talk. Think about Verizon's "Can Your Hear Me Now?" campaign. It established the brand as the most consistent and dependable cell phone service available.

Clarity tells the world why you matter. The best brands edit their communication down to its essence and speak to their audience in a language they can understand and emotionally connect with. Think about how much American Express communicates with the simple tagline, "Take Charge."

Authenticity gives your brand staying power. Great brands come across as real. They don't manipulate the truth to get what they want. What they say about themselves comes directly from their true essence. Think of powerful brands like Starbucks, Zappo's, Google and Apple. Not only do they have authenticity at their core, their visual image syncs up with what they say they can do.

When you throw dirt, you'll lose ground and that will kill your reputation in the process.

My issue with Trump and so many other grandstanders, false prophets and arrogant ladder-climbers is that underneath their spitfire rhetoric is a pack of lies. They may initially steal center stage, but will quickly become a sideshow. Here's how to not let that happen to you!

- Take a hard look at your own inconsistencies

- Stop letting things slide in your personal life and at work

- Start today by unearthing your true essence and find your best intentions

- Articulate your brand's mission – its purpose in the world

- Harness your creative energy behind your mission

Even well established business leaders and celebrities like Trump misplace or forget their purpose. They are so busy trying to win sales, ratings or votes that they go off track and confuse their audience. When that happens, loyalty dies.

False truths and denial have become an epidemic in America. It hangs juries and leaves our children questioning what integrity really means. To stave off this ethical breakdown, we have to hold our leaders and ourselves to a higher standard. You can start right now by imagining what the world would look if all of us were real in business and model that behavior in your own career.

When you compromise the truth, you risk your own serenity and the value you bring to the world.

What Business Are You In?

Figuring out the answer to this important question will give you the competitive edge.

A couple of years ago I was guiding a bio-medical company toward unearthing the soul of their brand— when suddenly the CEO realized that his company wasn't in the *pain relief business* – it was actually in the *patient empowerment business.* This aha! moment led us down a previously-unimagined path to expansion.

I'm sure that when Coke grasped that they were in the *happiness business* a major opening occurred. The same is probably true for American Express who sees itself as more than a credit card service, but a club where members receive desirable rewards. Similarly, Southwest's competitive advantage lies in its realization that it's not in the *travel business,* but in the *customer service business.*

If I had limiting beliefs for my own company – thinking that it was merely an advertising agency or branding firm, we would have died a long time ago. Knowing that we were in the *potential fulfillment business* gave us our true purpose – a deeper meaning that makes what we do relevant in any economy and for any type of client.

Whether you are in charge of a corporate brand, small business brand or your own brand, you must look past your product or service and find its soul.

To figure out what business you are really in, follow these three steps:

Step One: Gather Some Insights

Contact ten clients or key influencers and ask them why they buy from you and/or like to do business with you. What is it about the product or service that you deliver that sets you apart from the rest?

Step Two: Make A List Of Top Brands

Look at your research findings and think of major brands that you admire that share these same qualities. Write down five of those brands and what business they are in.

Step Three: Look Deeply Into What You Do

Great brands have meaning beyond their names that create emotional connections. Knowing this, look at what you do with fresh eyes, redefine what business you are in and adjust the way you compete accordingly.

Let's say you own a chain of successful bakeries. Knowing that you are in the *comfort business*, how will you cater to your customer's need to feel comfortable? If you have a coaching practice and you now realize that you are in the *high performance business,* how will make your clients accountable? If you are the head of human resources at a major corporation and you realize that you are in the *sensitivity business,* what steps will you take to understand and inspire your employees?

Taking the time to understand what business you are really in will expand your vision and at the same time sharpen your career focus.

Turning Your Uniqueness Into Your Advantage

Being different is a major positive if you leverage what's unique about you to achieve your higher purpose.

Sometimes I feel so different it hurts. On the one hand, I know it's a good thing to think differently, dress differently, and be raised differently. It sets me apart and in a crowded marketplace, and that's a plus. On the other hand, swimming against the tide can be very exhausting and downright scary! I'm flying solo in so many circumstances – transcending every fear to find a place within me that can turn on compatibility and find connection – I often feel lost upon landing.

Fear. It keeps us from telling the truth to our clients, picking up the telephone (instead we hide behind email), and actually calling a prospect we are dying to work with or asking for the money we are worth. We don't want to ruffle feathers, upset the apple cart or worse, be seen as weird. We desire to fit in, be liked or even loved, performing for applause that only comes in the form of a late payment. We want to change, finally be ourselves, but how?

Perhaps you are perceived as someone who doesn't fit in or you're considered outside the norm, or some may feel that you're too controversial. You're considered ahead of your time, maybe even an iconoclast. Whatever you are, you don't run with the pack; instead, you march to the beat of your own drum.

If I've just described you, count your blessings. You are indeed fortunate. Your natural characteristics are what will—and likely, already have—set you apart in a positive way. You may not feel very positive about those differences right now because you've been busy trying to wish them away or cover them up. The truth is, if you stand out not because you're different, but because you're solidly grounded in who you are—with no apologies – you'll be the Steve Jobs-Oprah-Ellen-Einstein of your world. And how great would that be? Marinate in that thought for a minute – feels good, doesn't it?

If you can get out of the despair of being the only one like you, you'll find that people will gravitate toward you because of your energy, confidence, and flair. None of us comes into this world with a handbook to guide us in developing our personalities. We simply jump into life and do the best we can. But what if you feel different— that you somehow don't fit in with the norm, that you aren't truly recognized and accepted for who you are? Trying to retrofit yourself into society and work life can be daunting, burning you out before you've even had a chance to shine.

If there is one thing I've learned, it's that acting out of fear and living according to other people's needs will pigeonhole you into being someone you're not, and that's not what life is about. Our job is to be open to the possibilities and see how far we can go. Life is a journey, so why not make the most of it? So, let's begin the journey of celebrating your distinctiveness.

It is a lifelong process to get to know and accept ourselves as different.

One of my closest friends recently said to me, "What if I've come this far and I still don't know who I am?" As much as we want to quickly understand ourselves, there are no shortcuts to the truth. We're deep and multifaceted, and we're changing all the time. But at our core—in our souls—we are stable, vibrant beings with philosophies, values, and perspectives that travel with us throughout our lives.

Open up to your authentic self. Sounds scary, huh? "The real me?" Sometimes we're not quite sure who that is. When we're used to feeling distant from the group, we tend to submerge our true selves in an effort to be accepted. The real movers and shakers in this world live their lives with conviction; they rarely hide who they are. They accept that they were born different or landed in circumstances that make them different, and they embrace the opportunity to stand out from the pack. We all have that same opportunity.

If you're different, you already attract attention. The good news is attracting attention may be the best thing that ever happened to you!

Step 6:
Leave A Bad Situation

When your workplace culture or situation isn't the right fit, leave with grace and without burning bridges. Avoid getting into the blame game, or lost in details and gossip. Let go of resentment. You deserve to be happy!

In this step you will learn to:

Find Out Where You Fit

Stop Going Undercover

Leave Gracefully

Are You In The Wrong Business?

If you're trying to squeeze yourself into being someone you're not, it's time to reinvent yourself.

At business school, they teach a class called "Organizational Behavior." During this class, you learn that there are two different kinds of people in business: Clock Builders and Time Tellers. To run— the world needs both kinds of people – those who create the vision (Clock Builders) and those who can execute it (Time Tellers). Knowing which role you play best is essential to career fulfillment and happiness.

I am, without a shred of doubt, a Clock Builder. Yet not long ago, I played the role of a Time Teller, and it took its toll on me.

I was living in Los Angeles, riding the Internet wave and making millions. Big Fish was creating launch campaigns for television series like *Lost, Desperate Housewives, Top Model,* and *Project Runway.* We were the go-to agency for any major television event, including the Olympics and the Academy Awards.

It only took a few years of living on crushing deadlines for me to realize that I was building the wrong business. My unique talent was in creating world-class brands, yet most days I was stuck writing headlines for banner ads. I had lost my North Star — I was off mission and fulfilling someone else's purpose— not mine.

Don't strive for success— strive to create meaning when you reinvent yourself.

I know how tempting it can be to let your career happen to you. Money can be a powerful distraction. But in the end, you have to measure your career not by a monetary meaning of success, but by the difference you are making in the world.

If you've gotten off track and strayed away from your true calling, ask yourself these questions to determine if you're in the wrong business.

___ Do you feel you're not working in your passion?

___ Are you undervalued or under-utilized somehow?

___ Is the culture of your workplace not a good fit for you?

___ Do you tell your friends and family, "I'm in it for the paycheck?"

___ Does your boss put you down or pass you over for promotions?

___ Is your job a demoralizing experience?

___ Do you question your own abilities, capacities, or perceptions?

___ Do you feel like all you ever do is throw in the towel?

___ Are your suggestions met with a patronizing response?

___ Is there a lack of acceptance because you look or sound different?

___ Do you dread going to the office and wish you could dash it all?

If your answer was "Yes" to two or more questions, perhaps it's time for you to redirect your career or business towards something you are passionate about – something that you can do that really matters.

Only a few years ago, my company was at the nexus of entertainment and interactive advertising. Many of the clients we had are still with us today, but the projects they bring are in the Clock Builder realm. And because of this, the work is vastly more rewarding and satisfying to me.

When you reinvent yourself, remember that it doesn't matter how good the money is if you're not living your true purpose.

Why Going Undercover Is A Self-Esteem Killer

Don't fool yourself. If you are someone's "secret weapon," you're being undervalued.

I'll never forget the time I received a phone call on a Friday from a client who needed a messaging strategy delivered by noon on Monday. She expected gold in that timeframe, and I was determined to give it to her. I was going to save the day where my competitor had failed, and craft the right words to ignite an entire sales team.

It was a suicide mission. Why do it? Well, the money was a factor, but it wasn't my entire reason for taking the project. I wanted to prove my worth to a client who had not hired me in a few years and remind her how smart I was. Looking back, I can see that my motivation was mostly ego-driven and my intention lacked integrity.

Bringing me in was a political hot potato. I was told that my involvement would have to be top secret. I was hired to save the day, but no one could know I was actually doing the work. Wanting to prove myself, I climbed aboard promising to hit the target like a stealth fighter pilot.

I worked like mad over the weekend to produce a winning strategy. On Monday when I presented it to my client, I received a lukewarm reception.

I was angry with myself for taking the project, for agreeing to be invisible, for working over the weekend, taking time away from my family and for thinking that what I had created was so great that it would blow them away. Was I simply in love with my own work to the point of delusion? Perhaps.

Looking back, I could have done one of two things to prevent this: 1) refuse the project or 2) take it and say, "I'll do this, but you realize that I have a process that is proven and without it, I can't guarantee a positive outcome." Either of those paths would have kept me from feeling like a failure.

When someone wants to hide your involvement or take credit for your work, think twice about how it might harm your personal brand and your self-esteem.

In the end, I listened to my client's feedback and turned in a revised strategy the next day that made her very happy. She would take credit for my work and possibly give credit to my competitor. I would be forever branded her "Work Mistress."

A couple of weeks later I visited my business coach and regurgitated the story. As I was talking, I flashed back to when I was a student at the University of Alabama. I remembered a frat boy from the Phi Gam house that treated me like a mistress – never taking me to parties or football games – only to quiet restaurants across town where no one would find us. Somewhere in the back of my mind I knew he was ashamed to be with me because I was Jewish. I just wanted to be at his table without having to admit to myself that he was marginalizing me with every clandestine date.

Over the past 20 years, there have been a number of times when I've played that same role in business. Each time I agree to go undercover, I stop myself from stepping into my power and living my true purpose. Just like a foolish woman who thinks that being a mistress will lead to marriage, my willingness to be invisible tells the world that I am second rate when I am so much more than that.

Being invisible, behind-the-scenes, under-the-radar... call it what you will... if your work is being hidden, your personal brand will be diminished.

How to Leave a Bad Work Situation Gracefully

Is it time to change a career and seek greener pastures?

In 2006 my company was hired to create a brand strategy and marketing plan for a new venture backed by KISS front man Gene Simmons. The project entailed branding a television network and website that featured uncensored music videos.

At first I was excited. I had been a concert promoter in college and early in my career I was in the music business—first as a marketing manager at a large record store chain and then as a promotion director at a pop radio station in Atlanta.

What I had forgotten was how dysfunctional the music business could be, and Gene's company was no exception. Sexual innuendo and derogatory comments marked the executive's exchanges with each other and with me. It wasn't a match—I was off my path, walking down memory lane instead of striding boldly into my future.

After putting in three months on a lucrative six-month contract, I thought about walking away. My involvement just didn't feel right. But, I was in business to make money, and I agonized over the loss of revenue. In the end, I concluded that no amount of money was enough for me to sell my soul. So I met with each executive individually, delivered parting gifts, and explained honestly that I just couldn't do my best work in this environment.

If you no longer can stand the thought of showing up for work and you're doing it for the paycheck, it's time to walk.

It takes courage to say "no," to walk away, to make a change. After all, not knowing what's coming next can be frightening. On the other hand, I've never known change not to be for the better. Even when it's challenging, change forces you to look at yourself and decide what you really want. Change keeps you from growing complacent and getting stuck. It's a chance to reinvent yourself or explore new territory. It may not always be your choice, but it will almost always be for the best.

Making a change could mean leaving money on the table or moving to another location entirely; sometimes, we need to have the courage to disappoint people when the culture or situation isn't the right fit.

The worst thing you can do is beat yourself up or see yourself as a failure. Instead, you want to learn and grow from the situation, leave with grace and without burning bridges, show appreciation, and avoid getting into the blame game, or lost in details and gossip.

When you close the door behind you, make sure you leave behind any negative memories and emotions. Don't take the old baggage to the next job; make a fresh start. By resigning properly, you will be respected, and you will leave a positive legacy of your work.

What you do for a living shouldn't be something you tolerate. It should motivate you to become the person you truly are at your highest potential. If that's not happening in your current position, it may be time to KISS it goodbye.

Isn't it time you took the steps to change a career or let go of a negative work situation? You deserve to be happy!

Step 7:
Travel To Find
Yourself

Want to be more inspired at work? Travel. To experience a career rebirth, you have to leave the office. Make your journey a fearless expedition to the soul and you'll discover who you really are, and what you want to do next.

In this step you will learn to:

Become Inspired By Travel

Fit In Without Blending In

Carve Out "Block Time"

Want To Be More Inspired At Work? Travel.

To experience a career rebirth, you have to leave the office.

One summer, I traveled through Italy the entire month of June. I hiked the Cinque Terre, sipped delicious wine in the Lakes Region, and lived like a

Roman in a 14th century palazzo near Campo de'
Fiore.

Since starting my business 20 years ago, I've
made a commitment to spend the greater part of
June travelling outside the USA. I know this seems
counterintuitive to many Americans who take pride
in never taking time off, but I feel strongly that
travel is not an indulgence, but rather an essential
component of being a creative thinker and business
leader.

*Travel, unlike anything else in life, will inspire
you to master your area of interest and bring
more of yourself to the world.*

During my journeys, I discover who I really am
and what I want to do next. The great art I see, the
food I taste, stores I shop in, and people I meet
inspire me. With a passionate desire to live a life
rich in meaning, I find the possibilities in the
mystery of *what will happen next* that only travel
delivers.

For example, as a student and teacher of
reinvention, I couldn't help but be inspired by
Florence, the birthplace of the Renaissance. The
word *renaissance* actually means "rebirth"— that
period of great cultural change that followed the
dreary and overbearing dark ages.

During the Renaissance, rediscovering the past
became the key to understanding the future. From
Leonardo da Vinci to Michelangelo to William

Shakespeare, great men peeled back the layers of time to spark scientific, artistic, business and civic achievement.

Travel shouldn't be about leaving or running away; it's about finding you.

Like the great Renaissance masters who looked to the Ancient Greeks and Romans for inspiration, I discover my own roots when I travel. Whether visiting Hungary to see where my ancestors once lived or going to Israel to learn about the seeds of my faith, my self-esteem grows and my creativity flourishes when the journey takes me back.

You may be reading this thinking, "but if I get away so and so may get that promotion" or "I can't afford to take time off, I could lose business." Here's how I keep those fears from becoming a reality.

Get Rid Of Dead Weight

Before you go, fire anyone that you cannot count on to work hard for you during your absence. Stop fooling yourself into thinking that they'll rise to the occasion. They won't. Chances are without you watching, they'll piss off your top client and destroy your reputation. I speak from experience here.

Get Out Of Your Time Zone

If it's possible for you financially, leave the country. Then people will understand that you are going to be difficult to reach and they won't expect an immediate return of phone calls or emails.

Bring Your Laptop

Get up in the morning and work for a couple of hours. Then again before you go to bed. In between, live your life and love every minute, smartphone-free.

Journal Everything That Inspires You

Write down or use a recorder to journal any thoughts that come up about your business. I am constantly seeing things or hearing things that inspire me to bring something new to my work.

Toss Out Your Limiting Beliefs

I have always had a lot of fear around heights and things going really fast. When my daughter suggested that we visit Costa Rica, I challenged myself to zip-line over the rainforest canopy, rappel down waterfalls and drive an ATV through rushing rivers. I made it home safe and sound and very proud of myself.

There's a big world out there and it's time for you to see it. Vow to have your own personal Renaissance. See your vacation as an expedition to your soul and you'll find your way to mastering life and business.

You've got to get out to get in. Become a traveler to unearth a deeper connection to your work.

How To Fit In Without Blending In

Getting too entrenched in the culture can make you lose hold of yourself and that can be a reputation killer!

While aboard a train travelling from Milan to Rome, I couldn't help but think about the expression "When in Rome," which means to act like a local when you're in a foreign situation. Does this wisdom apply if you've joined a new company or moved to a new city or started work in a new industry? I think it does, but only to a point.

Every time I take on a new client, I have to completely immerse myself in their world. I interview all the top executives, learn to speak their language and operate like one of the team. However, because I'm tasked with finding out what's working and what's not in order to reignite my client's brand, I have to maintain my perspective.

When my nephew Jori graduated from Northwestern, he decided to take a job at a start-up in San Francisco as a software engineer. He knew that to be successful, he'd have to adopt a West Coast mindset and operate like a dotcom entrepreneur. At the same time, he brought his Midwestern work ethic, unique style and bold way of thinking to the job. The combination boded well for him as he received more and more responsibility and recognition. In less than 18 months, Jori was lured away by another start-up that offered him a bigger title and a much higher salary – by fitting in without blending in, Jori made his mark.

To find your way in, embrace aspects of the culture that resonate with your personal brand.

Here are three things you must do to master this balancing act and what you'll need to do the next time you find yourself in a new situation:

1. Be A Cultural Detective

Your detective work should begin before you ever enter the culture. If you are going for a new job, visit the company's website or Wikipedia page, study its products, people and mission statement, and read about its vision. Once you land the position or project, locate the company historian, the one who's been there for years. Take that person to lunch and ask questions about the company, its policies, and its culture. Explain that you want to make a difference, and ask for advice.

2. Hold On To Your Style

Giving up your look can be like giving up your soul. That's why when I go to a business meeting or give a speech I consider my audience and dress in a way that is respectful to them. When I'm in the South, I wear color. While in New York, I'm in a black dress or suit. On the West Coast jeans and a jacket. No matter the area or the type of business, I make sure to accessorize in a way that lets people know I'm creative and worldly. It's important to adhere to customs and even embrace them as your own as long as you don't change so much for others that you no longer recognize yourself in the mirror.

3. Make Some Waves

When I was in my 20s, I would get into a new job and immediately want to change the company overnight. However, when I got to Turner Broadcasting, I found that things moved slowly and there was less flexibility. Luckily, I had a boss who taught me how to *choose my battles wisely*. Instead of being seen as a rebel, I chose projects that would define the brands I represented, and in turn build my reputation as an innovator. Having this kind of filter will keep you on a career path that brings you recognition.

When you enter a new situation that's not familiar, make sure that you maintain your individuality within the existing culture. Being too much of an outsider will keep you from making a positive difference. Being too much of an insider will diminish your creativity. Bottom line... when in Rome, do like the Romans, but don't lose yourself in their world.

Remember who you are and what you stand for so that you don't dilute your personal appeal and impact.

When You Need To Get It Done, Get Away!

Stop putting off all the important things you want to do and give yourself some block time.

When I tell people that I write a weekly blog, have several training programs completed, a series of keynote speeches ready to give, and four books under my belt, they inevitably say, "That's amazing, how do you do it all?" I say, "I give myself *block time.*"

What is block time? It's making creative space for yourself away from your job, your family and your social commitments to give a block of uninterrupted time to the endeavors that express your personal brand and are aligned with your mission.

If you're looking for a new job, you're ready to change jobs, or you want to impress higher-ups, you could use the time to refresh your resume, bio and LinkedIn page, create a presentation detailing a big idea that you want to bring to your boss, outline a book, draft a Ted Talk, start a Twitter account or build a Facebook fan page.

The space to do your great work will never find you, you have to carve it out and be protective of it.

When I told a friend that I was traveling to The Mabel Dodge Luhan House in Taos, NM for two days to write this book he was envious. Even though I was only driving one hour north of my home in Santa Fe, he sighed and said, "I wish I could get away like that." He just couldn't imagine drawing a boundary and making all the arrangements needed to peel away for a couple of days – even if it would end up increasing his perceived value and feeding his soul.

Luckily, I've learned not to put roadblocks up where there aren't any. So here I sit in the reading parlor of a home that was once owned by Dennis Hopper, where luminaries like D.H. Lawrence, Georgia O'Keefe and Ansel Adams frequented, seeking their help from beyond, to inspire these words. I take long walks in the mornings, eat meals alone with my thoughts and explore the interior of my mind for messages that will motivate you to fearlessly achieve your highest potential, so that I can reach mine.

Taking time to do your life's work is not selfish; it's why you are here.

If I'm inspiring you to finally get the block time you need, but you just don't know exactly how to ask for it from your partner or boss, here are a couple of scripts I've cooked up that might get you a day or two away.

For Your Life Partner/Spouse

"Honey, you know how you keep telling me that I really need to write my (fill in the blank)? Well, I feel compelled now more than ever to do it! It's all bottled up inside of me and I'm ready to let it out. But here's the thing: instead of doing it piecemeal, I feel I need a serious block of time to really get it done. I've found this little bed and breakfast one hour away where I can just be with my work for a couple days. While I'm gone, I have arranged play dates for the kids and the teenager next door will walk the dog. Just imagine, you'll have time for yourself to catch up on your (fill in the blank) and I'll get my project off the ground, finally."

For Your Boss

"For some time you've been recommending that I become more visible outside of our department and inside our industry. You've asked that I enhance my profile and perception so that I can be seen as a leader. I really appreciate all of your advice and I've taken it to heart. The thing is, my job here requires all of my time and I'm unable to (fill in the blank), as you've suggested. I've found this little bed and breakfast one hour away where I can just be with my work for a couple days. I would like permission to block out the time so I can get away from all the urgent tasks here to take care of those important projects that will not only benefit my image, but the entire department. While I'm gone, I have arranged for (name of employee) to pitch in. Just imagine, I'll finally get (fill in the blank) off the ground and you'll be able to show (name of head honcho) how you motivated me to reach my potential."

Now, if your boss is an ass and he or she doesn't want you to succeed, you can still getaway from your home or the office and grab some block time close by. You can simply spend a Saturday or Sunday at Starbucks or some other Wi-Fi infused coffee house drinking lattes with your cell phone locked away in your glove box. I do it all the time, and I even surprise myself at the amount of work I get done.

There's always going to be urgent matters standing in the way of what's important. Don't wait another minute. Plan your block time today!

Step 8:
Get Your Swagger Back

Having a No-Fear Career means showing up to work courageously. To get to that place of strength, think back to when you aced a presentation, won a project, received an honor or captured a major piece of business. Bring this energy and confidence into the room and you'll be well on your way to getting your swagger back.

In this step you will learn to:

Express Yourself Confidently

Move From Doubt to Clarity

Find Your Signature Style

Make a Powerful Presentation

Celebrate You!

6 Sure-Fire Ways To Get Your Swagger Back

How To Conjure Up Confidence When You're Off Your Game

I'll never forget the day I was working out at the gym passively watching CNN on the wall in front of me. Suddenly, there he was on the screen... George Clooney. It was a replay of the actor-activist's press conference at the White House when he spoke about Sudan. I couldn't hear a word he was saying, and it didn't matter. His swagger said it all.

What is swagger? It's a confident way of moving that non-verbally says, "Pay attention, what I do and what I have to say matters." Clooney's swagger mixes humble with cocksure ease like nobody's business.

Before the recession, many of you had Clooney-like swagger. You would walk into a room like a CEO and make things happen. You knew who you were; and told yourself you could do anything. Then, it all changed. Some of you lost customers or got taken down a peg with a pink slip. In what felt like a blink of an eye, you were brooding instead of producing – shell shocked instead of firing away.

I've been there, and I have to tell you there are ways to raise your self-esteem and get your swagger back, and get it back better than before. Swagger and charisma go hand in hand. Think of Kate Middleton when she strides out into the public, cool and collected. Wow! Before she flashes that dazzling smile and queen-like luster, I can imagine her telling herself, "I'm beautiful, confident and loved." Self-talk is a big component to getting your swagger back.

Even if you lost it, you can raise self esteem and get your swagger back today. here's how:

STAND TALL. Height communicates authority. If you're tall, accentuate it, own it and for goodness sake, don't slouch. If you're not tall, practice moving with confidence and wearing clothing that's tailored to fit you. A clean line from head to toe gives the appearance of stature.

WALK RIGHT IN, SIT RIGHT DOWN. When you enter a room, don't hesitate in the doorway or bashfully poke your head in. Remember: you belong! And if you have a choice, choose any upright chair over a sofa, which can swallow you up in a single gulp.

PASSIONATELY ENGAGE. Know these expressive tools: Wide eyes demonstrate interest. A very gentle nod indicates understanding, agreement, and approval. When you lean forward, your intensity and passion come across. It goes without saying that a gesture doesn't substitute for what it represents, but with practice, using these positive and powerful physical communicators can become a natural way of expressing interest, understanding and passion.

LISTEN TO YOURSELF. Sit down with a tape recorder and talk. Then play it back. How did you do? Do you sound confident or fragile? Try lowering your voice down an octave and speaking from your diaphragm. Clooney and celebrities like Jennifer Lopez and Martha Stewart do this. Like them, you'll be taken more seriously when you do.

EVALUATE YOURSELF AS A STORYTELLER. Grab a friend and tell him or her how you see yourself. Unspool a story about your life. Again, make a recording. Listen for ums, ers, you knows and other hesitations. Listen for word tics, words that you overuse. Do you sound stilted? Does your enthusiasm and confidence come across in your voice?

SPEAK WITH A SMILE. We are living in a time where business relationships can go on for years without ever a face-to-face meeting. So knowing how to communicate swagger in your tone is essential. If you smile when you answer the phone, your smile will shine right through the lines. If you're smiling, you'll sound as if you couldn't be more delighted to be talking to the person on the other end. An upbeat personality communicates self-assuredness, personal comfort, and a positive outlook.

Swagger comes from a place deep inside of you. Access it by remembering who you really are in your highest self.

To reconnect with your swagger, go back in time to when you aced a presentation, won a project, received an honor or captured a major piece of business. Now, stand tall, speak with authority and smile ear-to-ear from that place of strength. You'll find your self-esteem growing as you quietly say to yourself, "Clooney, step aside."

It's You Dude, Snap Out Of It!

If you're not getting calls returned, your salary increased or a seat at the table on cool projects, check yourself.

So many people I know who once had major success in high profile positions now feel like they can't get even get a phone call returned. One former television executive just asked me, "Am I pathetic?"

When you question yourself in this way, you don't show up, uncertainty does. You may think you're fooling everyone with the right clothes and your *game face*, but your insecurity is all they see.

Feeling like you are not enough or that nothing you do is enough is an old story that has a lousy ending.

Confidence and enthusiasm is what you need to exude in business. Today's decision makers want to be reassured that they are making the right choice by working with you. There's a lot of doubt in the business world and when you doubt yourself, you just add to it.

Here are five ways to step away from doubt and uncertainty and get righteous with the real you:

Connect With A Supportive Community.

Community creates contentment. That's why it's important not to isolate. When we separate ourselves from our feelings and from positive influences, we sabotage our happiness. To connect with your highest self, get into a group that meets regularly and say "goodbye" to people who don't believe in you.

Get Your Swagger On.

It bears repeating, to instill confidence in yourself and others, you have to move in a way that tells people, "Pay attention to me. What I do and have to say matters." Make a list of all of your accomplishments to remind yourself of how talented and valuable you really are and then read that list right before you make an important call or walk into a meeting.

Be Cooperative, Not Competitive.

Yes, you have to stand out from the pack to get a great job or make an awesome deal. Just don't be ugly about it— when you throw dirt, you lose ground. You want to be seen as a relationship builder who works well with others and can motivate a team to excellence – someone who can collaborate and co-create with a lot of different personalities.

Stop Asking Everyone What They Think.

Let's face it, you're not seeking advice, you're seeking approval. And the more advice you get, the more confused you become. The answers are inside of you. Listen carefully to your gut and let it guide you to what you really want.

Communicate With Yourself Authentically.

More than ever, people are in fear and they want to be around those with inner strength. Now is the time to know yourself, be sure of yourself and stop apologizing for who you are. If you can't see past your failures, start being conscious in each moment so you can feel the goodness in you.

The purpose of all communication is love, not judgments or manipulation. Check your motivations. If you're coming from a place of desperation, scarcity or vindictiveness, stop right there and do something to take care of you. Go for a long walk, volunteer, have a good meal, get a massage or play with your children. You'll find that through self-care your attitude will improve and opportunity will come knocking.

Remember, before you can be real with others, you have to draw in and get real with yourself.

Why What You Wear To Work Really Matters

Let's face it, judgments are made the minute you walk through the door.

I have a friend who is very smart, very charming, and very New York. At my suggestion, he interviewed for a sales position at Turner Networks in Atlanta. After the interview I asked the head of sales how the interview had gone. "He did two things wrong," he said. "What was that?" I asked. "He wore cuff links. Too affected. And I never trust a man in pleated pants."

Maybe appearances shouldn't count, and maybe people shouldn't be allowed to pass judgments based solely on how someone is dressed, but it happens everyday.

In any business situation, appearances count big time.

Dressing for success today is about reflecting your authentic self in a way that attracts your target audience. In other words, your clothes should not disguise who you are inside, they should communicate the essential stuff that makes you *you* at a glance.

Think about what's on the shelves of your local supermarket. If a product is a trusted brand, a customer will toss it in the shopping cart without a thought. But if it's brand new, if she notices it at all, she's likely to look at the package and be positively – or negatively influenced by everything that went into designing it: the shape of its box, its graphics, colors, typeface, and so forth. The package is a powerful tool that if used correctly, can influence a customer to buy.

When packaging your own personal brand, the exact same rules apply. Your audience is going to be consciously and unconsciously influenced by your appearance. In addition to how you put yourself together, you'll be evaluated on what your business card looks like, the paper stock of your resume, your portfolio, and your website. All of these parts comprise your package.

Your clothes and everything that visually reflects you should express your creative energy, your talent, your warmth, your way of thinking, your expertise.

Here's how to create a look that distinguishes you from the pack and makes a great impression:

Do Your Research: Be A Wardrobe Detective

In advance of any meeting, walk through the lobby of the building you'll be visiting during lunch time and observe everyone's style as they pass by. If that's not possible, google your prospect and find a profile picture or visit the company website or Facebook page for employee images.

Hamburgers or Caviar? Consider Your Audience's Taste.

After you've done your research, think about what your target audience will respond to, feel safe with, understand, respect and admire. Then consider how you can fit in to their culture without blending in.

Establish A Signature Style That's Memorable

If you are in a creative industry, look creative. I won my biggest account wearing a pair of jodhpurs, a riding jacket with a man's tie boldly printed with a cowboy busting a bronco.

Look Current Even if Your Industry Is Conservative

What's important is to feel confident, secure and savvy. You don't want to copy anyone. Wear clothes that tell your target you are capable of just about anything, especially moving up.

Get Your Clothes Tailored, Your Shoes Re-heeled.

Take a tip from the top CEOs, always tailor your clothes to fit beautifully and make sure to keep your shoes in shape uneven heels are a sign of disrepair. They communicate someone who's going down, not up and coming.

Discover Your Signature Piece

The writer Tom Wolfe was known for his white suits, Diane Keaton lives in turtlenecks and huge belts; Johnny Depp wears a fedora. Choose a distinctive accessory or "recognizer" and make it your own.

Dare to be a professional with real style. Whether you're powerful, glamorous, retro, super sleek or funky, you'll signal to the world that you are a confident and creative leader.

Make A Presentation That Sticks

Your presentation style should project a long-term, going-somewhere brand that's all about success.

Years ago at a Turner Broadcasting off-site meeting in Arizona, I was asked to demonstrate how we were motivating our cable affiliates to advertise TNT at the local level. This was not especially scintillating material. Basically, we sent out a monthly support kit with print and television ads that affiliates could customize. The more ads they ran, the more points they received that translated into prizes (read: we bribed them.)

My challenge was to make walking through this kit exciting to a room of 100 people in shorts dying to get poolside. I borrowed my girlfriend's red strapless ball gown and long white opera gloves and threw on gobs of rhinestones. I entered from the back of the room like Queen Elizabeth— head high, gaze straight ahead. I held the kit in my hands as if it were the Holy Grail. Meanwhile, champagne was being passed to everyone there.

When I got to the front of the room, I turned around and announced, "Welcome to a *formal* presentation of the Turner Affiliate Kit." Jaws dropped and ears opened.

Research shows that visuals count for more than half the emotional impact of any presentation. It's not just what you say, but how you present it visually that counts.

Another time I was asked to lead a panel discussion on how to create "effective promotion partnerships" – as when McDonald's puts the latest toy from a kid's movie inside their Happy Meals.

Instead of creating a boring PowerPoint, I presented a "promotion cocktail." I put on an apron, rolled out a bar cart and started squeezing oranges as I talked about "the juiciest ideas." Next, I poured the juice into a martini shaker and added fine sugar to demonstrate "sweetening the deal." Then I poured vodka "to get the contract signed." Finally, I shook the shaker and served the drink to my panelists—in glasses that sported my company's Big Fish logo. (Never stop branding!)

This level of creativity has characterized the way I have done business for 20 years, and it's one of the reasons that great brands like Sony, Disney and MTV keep coming back to work with Big Fish year after year. We just make branding and marketing look like fun.

Speaking is a *contact sport.* It's all about connecting with your audience. Real credibility happens when you get comfortable speaking to large groups of people. It's amazing how you transform yourself into a brand leader when you stand up in front of a group solidly and add a bit of pizazz. And that's just the perception you need to move up in the business world.

I really believe that anyone can learn to give an unforgettable presentation. From taking a night class and hiring a voice specialist to attending weekend workshops and bringing in a private presentation coach, I've done it all to hone my skills in this area.

Solid training can help you develop a signature presentation style that will give you an edge.

I'll never forget the time I left my portfolio on the train. As I walked out of Grand Central Station I began rehearsing how I'd open the meeting. I was eager and excited to meet with A&E's marketing team to show them why Big Fish was the right match for them. It wasn't until I walked into the boardroom and saw 10 executives looking at me down a long conference table that I realized that my portfolio was missing. I decided in that moment to ask everyone to play "Theatre of the Mind" with me. I saved the day by standing up and recalling each piece in my portfolio with zeal. I landed A&E as a client that day and received my portfolio back safely.

How can you make your next presentation unforgettable?

Celebrate You!

Feeling self-conscious? Doubting your value? It may be time to throw yourself a party.

I stretched out my last birthday over two weeks and milked the milestone for all it was worth. I attended intimate dinners and cocktail events that I arranged in my honor in Chicago, New York, Atlanta and Los Angeles. As I made my way across the country, each night I would walk into a room filled with people I love. In turn, the next day I came to my meetings happily in service.

Injecting more love into your life is essential to your success. That's because closing deals and building relationships is no longer about selling, it's about serving. We serve others when we bring love into the room – when we compassionately listen to their challenges and provide tailor-made solutions. This naturally happens when you leave your problems and ego at the door and operate with principled intention.

Getting to that self-assured place can be difficult— especially if you feel the weight of personal issues or you're caught up in a drama at work. To set all that aside and arrive from an authentic place of service, you have to know three things: 1) who you are, 2) the value that you bring to the table, and 3) how much you are loved.

After writing <u>Make A Name For Yourself</u>, my first book on personal branding, I was clear on who I was and what I brought to the table. However, as the years went on I felt less solid on the love part. Recognizing this, I decided to surround myself with people that I adore. My "birthday tour" did the trick to make me feel loved, grateful and truly happy.

How can you possibly be in service to others if you don't take care of yourself and ask for what you need?

Ultimately, people buy from people they love. How can you ever expect someone to promote you, partner with you, even listen to what you have to say if you doubt yourself or feel that you are not enough? Applying this idea of celebration to all that you are is essential to stepping away from fear and elevating yourself to a place of love and service.

Successful brands celebrate their stand out qualities and thrive on the loyalty they receive from their customers. Your personal brand requires no less from you than loyalty and a heartfelt celebration of your essence, all that you stand for and deliver. Bottom line: if you're sold on you then you can authentically communicate with passion and bring big love to everything you do.

Bring the love to you. Make a list of your favorite people and throw a party that reminds you how much you are loved.

Step 9:
Tell Your Greatest Story

Making a strong impression starts with being fearlessly authentic – not by performing or being emotionally manipulative. Proudly share your mission and your accomplishments in a way that serves others and you will instill confidence.

In this step you will learn to:

Make a Fantastic First Impression

Learn How To Tell A Great Story

Write Your Value Proposition

Say Just Enough

How To Make A Fantastic First Impression

When interviewing, tell your greatest story, not the whole story.

Many years ago when I was first building my business, I used to reveal way too much. The more insecure I felt, the more I would blabber on. This need to be heard was just one of the self-protections that had become part of my identity. I was a performer, and unconsciously I viewed everyone as my audience. I was convinced that if I could entertain them, I would win their approval, and thus their business.

I'll never forget being on a date with someone special. I was regaling him with stories about my college years – when he suddenly interrupted me and asked, "Will the real Robin Fisher please stand up?" I felt exposed, unsure of what to do next. Only moments earlier I'd felt confident and charming. This experience was a turning point in my life.

I slowly began to unpeel my performer layer and disciplined myself to ask questions and listen to the answers. The more present I was with my clients and my friends, the deeper the connections I was able to make. Through this transformation, I learned that I didn't need to perform to be loved or valued.

Creating executive presence requires you to make intelligent choices about what you reveal to those in your sphere of influence.

I have interviewed dozens of *unedited* people for positions at my company who describe in intimate detail their failed relationships, weaknesses and flaws. They are desperately seeking approval. What they are really saying is, "Hey this is absolutely the most hideous I can be. If you can accept it, we can work together."

On the other hand, I have interviewed people who are so overly self-conscious that they appear guarded. I end up thinking, "what are they hiding?" There has to be a balance. That's why when you're trying to make a great first impression, it's important to show yourself honestly the first time.

Here's how to use personal brand strategies to make a positive first impression in situations where you are being interviewed, you're auditioning, trying to win business or get promoted:

Do a 180-degree turn and stand in the shoes of the interviewer

They want to know why you are the right person to solve their challenges, and what proof you have that you can actually make their life easier and better their company's performance.

Share what you have going for you instead of what you're missing

There's no need to blurt out your list of wounds and weaknesses because you think that revealing them will somehow make others understand you. True alliances cannot be formed through manipulation or by soliciting sympathy.

Tell your greatest story (not the whole story)

If you want to shape or change perception, talk about how you triumphed in a difficult situation – what goals you set and met, how you turned things around, the ways you personally made a difference. Believe in yourself and you'll make a believer of others.

Ask smart questions and practice active listening to get the answers

Being curious is a sign of intelligence. Come armed with a list of questions that will spark a deeper conversation. Weave in your knowledge of the company and the person who's interviewing you to demonstrate that you're truly interested in their business.

Making a strong first impression starts with being authentic – not by performing or being emotionally manipulative. Your goal is to present your highest self and instill confidence in what you can do. And after all, isn't that what potential bosses, clients and customers want to see from you?

Telling your greatest story will reveal your true nature, which is an essential component in creating a personal brand.

Strategies For Responding To "Tell Me About Yourself"

It starts with telling a great story about your life where you played the superhero.

In the business of television, pitch meetings with network executives go pretty much the same way. If you are lucky enough to start in the president's office, the setting will be informal. He or she will invite you to the sofa and you'll do your presentation across a coffee table. The atmosphere will usually be pretty cozy and the vibe warm and friendly. After introductions, your prospective client will inevitably say, "Tell me about yourself and your company."

I always start at the very beginning – sharing that my dad was a single parent who taught my sister and me the ad business at an early age. Then I give a quick overview of my days working in radio, newspaper and finally television, where I helped launch TNT and turn CNN into *The World's News Leader*. To conclude my story, I walk everyone through a few relevant client case studies and share my branding philosophy and process.

Here's what I don't do: whine about not having a mom growing up, elaborate on personal challenges, complain about difficult clients, lie about my accomplishments, go off on tangents, diminish my talents, overstate what I could deliver or drone on without focus.

Building a captivating story about yourself involves sharing the epic moments in your life that reveal your true character.

To arrive at your answer to the question, "Tell me about yourself," it's important that you think deeply to uncover a time when you overcame adversity. This could be the beginning of your signature story – the one where you played the superhero. Michael Margolis, Dean of Story

University, talks about how most of us are reluctant or accidental heroes. He says, "Remember, you are not born a superhero. Superheroes are created based on circumstances and a choices." What were yours?

If you walk into a pitch meeting or give a presentation without a signature story and just go though the motions of showing your work, you'll miss making an emotional connection with your audience that will set you apart from your competition.

In addition to creating a signature story, it's important that you demonstrate that you're on a heroic quest. I always finish my story with my life's mission, which is to "help professionals fearlessly achieve their potential." I want my prospects to know that beyond delivering a transformational brand strategy, I am purposeful in my desire to inspire their employees.

If you want to play big and really make an impact in business, begin by sharing an epic story about yourself. The universe is waiting for you to proclaim your unique qualities. Your target audience wants to know that you can really make a difference to their organization.

When you reveal yourself through story, you honor your accomplishments and set the stage for your next triumph.

Here are some different forms of storytelling you can adopt courtesy of success guru Brendon Burchard:

Woe to win – when you were down and out, and then you came back

Finding or stumbling upon the magic bullet – and everything changed

David versus Goliath – when were you the underdog?

The tough choice – the other choice would've been easier, but this choice made you a better person

The switch from victim to victor – everyone has that story

The switch from self-absorbed to service minded – when was that point for you?

Family play – when did you decide that your family was important, and when did you sacrifice for them?

The no one believed I could do it story

The experience epic – 2-4 years of crap, then you came out of it a winner

The turnaround – when you finally decided to pursue something super meaningful

Start today writing a few different versions of your story and see which one makes you feel better about yourself. It should express what you were born to do and at the same time have a universal theme that everyone can relate to. In the end, your story should be one you feel proud to tell the world.

A quick note to those who are in the middle of a sad story: don't let your present circumstances define you. Think back to another time when you overcame a difficult situation and let that be your story for *right now*. The more you tell it, the more you'll start to believe that you are a superhero and you'll find yourself transitioning right into a happy ending.

If your story inspires you, it is sure to inspire others.

Go Ahead and Blow Your Own Horn

Declare your worth with a value proposition.

Last summer I gave a speech to a room full of television producers who were tired of being the best kept secret in Hollywood and wanted to step into the spotlight and become legendary brands like Jerry Bruckheimer, Tina Fey, Larry David and JJ Abrams. During the Q&A, someone asked me, "Shouldn't my work speak for itself?" I just had to laugh.

Look, maybe quietly toiling away could bring some recognition in the last century, but not in this one. Today you have to crisply define your value in a succinct, benefit-driven way that tells those in your sphere of influence why you and the work you do matters.

What I'm talking about is crafting a value proposition that comes from your highest self. These are the two or three sentences that you use at the beginning of every pitch, at your review, on your bio and LinkedIn profile and shrink down to 140-characters on Twitter. To make an unforgettable impression, your value proposition should contain your mission, unique skills and expertise and how those things serve the person or people you are trying to attract and influence.

When creating your value proposition, make sure that you are the solution to your audience's pain.

Whether you're a television producer selling to networks that struggle to increase ratings and solidify their brands, or you're a marketing executive at a major corporation challenged by your boss to engage customers, your job is to be the solution. *If you're not the solution, then you are irrelevant.* To create your own value proposition, think about your audience's pain points and the solutions you provide. If you're not sure what those points are, ask them to tell you their single biggest challenge. Then use these helpful tips to deliver your value in a way that solves their problem.

1. First, convey WHY you do what you do (a.k.a. your mission).

2. Share your point-of-view, i.e., "I believe that..."

3. Declare what is unique about you – how do you stand out?

4. Next, tell them how you're the solution to their pain.

5. Offer some credibility that gives them reasons to believe you.

6. Keep it simple – be conversational and don't use confusing terms.

7. Finally, make sure you whet their appetite so they'll want to hear more!

Here is an example of a value proposition for a project manager or outside consultant: "I am a collaboration catalyst. I believe that bringing people together to arrive at a solution creates buy-in and unifies the company towards a common goal. The magic happens when I pull together people from different areas of the organization and then lead the charge to move projects forward effectively and efficiently. My specialty is in helping to set and achieve goals with lightning speed, by welding radically different perspectives into a single team effort, avoiding wasted or dead-end thinking. I've demonstrated this unique skill at both Dell and IBM with astounding results and I know I can do it for you!"

Your value proposition should have the same confident tone as the example above. It must aim to serve, rather than sell. When you are finished saying it, there should be no mistake that you are a true asset and undeniable talent.

I learned long ago the power of taking charge of your perception to build your brand. In fifth grade, I sang, "I'm the Greatest Star" in front of my entire elementary school. My favorite lyric in that number is, *"I blow my horn until someone blows it."* Needless to say, I belted it out and haven't stopped since.

Speak for your work and hold yourself in high esteem – create a value proposition today!

When To Share It And When To Stuff It

It's not what you say, but how you say it that really matters.

After a few months into his new job, I met my nephew Jori in San Francisco for dim sum. Over barbeque pork buns and shrimp dumplings I asked him to tell me his single biggest challenge. He was quick to say, "Knowing when to share my opinions and when to shut up." Ah, yes. In that moment I knew he was kin to me in more ways than one.

Not long ago, I led a workshop for two merging media companies. My job was to find a common language that would glue them together in a meaningful way. I opened the workshop by underscoring the importance of our gathering – noting the latest research – which proves that in the absence of a cohesive culture, mergers can become train wrecks.

The next day, I received a phone call from one of the workshop participants telling me that my use of the phrase "train wreck" was disturbing. A few months later, the new regime let her go. Nonetheless, I learned that my delivery could have used some finesse.

The truth will set you free. Unless you open your mouth so many times, people stop listening.

This is your career and if the company you are working for or the client that's hired you is heading for a train wreck, it is your duty to let them know. However, the way you tell them is critical.

Get in the hot seat and tell your truth with passion using words and concepts that resonate. But remember to pick your battles carefully, know your audience's pain and have a solution for it.

Make what you have to say a real benefit, not a threat. Deliver your idea without judgment of yourself or others.

Step up to the plate. Grasp the bat of clarity firmly, and calmly set your sights. Before you swing, look inside to make sure your motives are grounded. If your focus is about connecting in a genuine way, then your objective is for the greater good. However, if what you're advocating involves a hidden agenda to gain power, prestige, or control over others, then you'll strike out.

Be mindful of your expectations. People will be people, and each will have individual responses that need to be taken into consideration. After all, judgment has become the social currency of our society. So be thoughtful and detached so that you are able to easily roll with the punches. The more you're invested in specific outcomes, the greater your disappointment will be if they don't work out as planned.

The big lesson here is to say what you need to say in a way that benefits your company or client. Make sure that you honor (not diminish) the people receiving your wisdom. If you are passionate about your ideas yet centered, you may be surprised by the impact you can make in the business world.

Pick your battles carefully and detach from the outcome. You'll find yourself operating from your highest good.

Step 10:
Get Off The Hamster Wheel

Budget and workforce cutbacks have caused many business leaders to fill multiple roles and juggle a multitude of projects at the same time. With demands on your time and resources coming in lightning fast, how can you stop going round and round with no end in sight?

In this step you will learn to:

Do Things Differently

Realize What You Really Value

Embrace Change

Stay Sane When It Gets Crazy

Ask For Help

How To Stop Bringing Your Work Home

What to do when you're overworked, overwhelmed and over-everything.

One beautiful Saturday afternoon, when I was still married, my husband climbed into our hot tub with me for a little soak. Steven had just come home from a 35-mile bike ride; I had just finished writing my blog.

I wanted to talk about my blog. Steven wanted to celebrate his glorious bike ride. He said, "Is there no sacred space for our relationship? Do we always have to talk about work? What about us?" Okay, good questions. Clearly, one of us was better at turning off work than the other (at least on the weekends.)

So instead of relishing the tranquility of the tub, we started to bicker and blame. Then somehow the conversation shifted to finding an answer to stopping the insanity. We were burned out not just on work, but talking about our business ad nauseam for 12 straight years since we had decided to join forces.

There, bathed in New Mexico sunshine and surrounded by juniper trees and Aspen-covered mountains, we came to realize that my weekend blog writing and our massive weekday to-do list left no room for our marriage.

Steven suggested that he'd make dinner on Monday nights while I write my blog. That way, we'd get to unplug, spend time together and fully engage with one another over the weekend. He was offering me block time (remember that concept?). I said, "Really? You would do that for me?" He said, "No, for us." Identifying the exact problem and coming up with a simple, but workable solution proved to be a major breakthrough for our relationship.

The only way to stop spinning out of control is to do things differently.

Although that Monday night solution couldn't solve every problem in our marriage or save our relationship from unraveling, I still have many happy memories of Steven preparing halibut baked in parchment paper or lemon chicken or grilled steaks, Simon and Garfunkel's concert in Central Park playing in the background, while I was sipping wine and writing my blog. Did I feel guilty because I wasn't helping him? Just a bit. But, I got over it!

In the work I do, I rarely meet a hard-driving business owner or executive who doesn't fantasize about getting off the hamster wheel. The exit strategy usually centers around having enough money socked away or getting the recognition they deserve. Just how much money or recognition is usually undefined and therefore, unattainable.

I have always been ambitious, but while soaking in the hot tub that day, I was forced to ask myself how much is enough and at what price. My drive at times could be toxic, especially when my fears surfaced and I fell into my defense mechanisms. When I would get overwhelmed, I would rattle off everything on my to-do list and feel like the weight of the world was on my shoulders. Sound familiar? I'll bet it does. Without openhearted compromise and fresh ideas, I would have kept going round and round like that and never moved forward.

These days I step back from the to-do list anxiety and self-imposed deadlines and take on each task one-by-one instead of looking at them as a massive burden that will never be lifted. It's not that I have less on my plate— I have a new attitude towards what needs to be done. Now when I feel pushed to the limit, I take care of myself by climbing into the hot tub, looking out at the mountains and enjoying the moment.

How will you leave your overwhelmed, overworked self behind to find space for yourself and your relationship?

Burned Out or Fired Up?

What would you rescue if your home suddenly caught fire? It could hold the key to your true career destiny.

I'm passionate about television. I have been since I was a little girl. When I was five years old our house caught on fire, and when my mother came in my room to rescue me, I rescued my little white portable Sony TV. I didn't have a favorite doll that I lavished love on. I adored my Sony instead.

Suze Orman tells a poignant story about a death-defying act that taught her the importance of money more vividly than any lesson. She was also a small child when her father's store caught fire, and he ran into his burning building to save the cash register, and carried it out, burning hot, in his bare arms. My devotion to my TV and its importance in my life felt like that.

Our house practically burned to the ground in our fire, and not very long after that my mom and dad split and I became a latchkey kid. Until my dad came home from work at night, it was pretty much the TV that kept me company. I tuned in to laugh, learn, and feel safe.

When I grew up, I became a television-marketing executive and for the past 20 years I have run a brand marketing firm that launches television shows and reinvents television networks. Sony is one of my most valued clients. Out of the ashes of that fire, my true destiny was determined.

What really makes you happy? What do you <u>love</u> to do? Who you are can be inferred from the things that interest you most. My client Werner Berger values courage. His passion is mountain climbing and it has propelled him to become the oldest person in the world to climb the highest peaks on all seven continents.

I think of values as having more <u>inner</u> significance, and passions as being more "of the world." For instance, one of my passions is cooking, which I can't claim to be something I value as much as I love, but cooking does say something about my desire to nurture the people I love, and is therefore a valuable clue to who I am.

Thousands of events, as big as a house fire, as small as a latchkey, go into forming who we are and what's important to us.

Every summer, devastating fires rip through New Mexico, Colorado and California, torching thousands of acres and forcing people to make difficult decisions about what to take with them as they evacuate their homes.

Whether you're burned out or fired up at work, take a moment to think about what you'd rescue from your home if it were threatened by fire. Beyond your life partner, kids and pets, make a record of those things you love most and just couldn't part with. It doesn't matter how many items you list.

This little assignment isn't designed to change who you are. It's about becoming self-aware and honest with yourself. It requires no judgments, just observation. But if you don't like what you see, it's within your power to make changes.

Your passions may be buried beneath a pile of work and responsibilities. Just for today, set them aside and dig deep to find the real you.

Embrace The Idea That Change Is Good

The Way To Live Deeply Is To Keep Reinventing Yourself

Over the past 18 years, my company has reinvented itself several times. In 1992, Big Fish opened its doors as a promotions firm handling sweepstakes and contests. In the mid-90's my company became a strategic branding firm. By the new millennium, we were in full swing as a digital advertising agency.

In sync with the ebb and flow of business, today the Big Fish tagline is "Reinventing Brands. Reigniting Professionals." With this positioning, I feel that I am closer to my true career destiny than ever before. I simply love the work I am doing, building major brands and helping people like you uncover your true purpose.

To thrive in business today, you have to embrace change. To live deeply, you have to evolve.

In his groundbreaking *Origin of the Species*, Charles Darwin wrote that, "Species . . . are still slowly changing by the preservation and accumulation of successive slight favorable variations." Fish, for example, started out as jawless filter feeders with bony armor over a cartilaginous body. Over thousands of years, they developed functioning vertebrae, gills, fins, and jaws— giving them a feeding advantage.

The nature of career evolution isn't much different: You need to periodically evaluate what's working for you and what isn't; be willing to preserve your indelible qualities and at the same time vary your look, your style and your thinking in a way that's advantageous to your situation.

In my case, I listen to my clients and the markets to find what's next and then take the classes or seminars necessary to master the skills needed to make the shift. For you, it may mean going on a sabbatical, volunteering, trying new sports, teaching a class, or learning a new language. It's time to think of what action you can take to reach your next peak and resist that doubting voice.

It's often adversity that spurs companies and people to greatness. Reinventing yourself is the answer.

Companies and people don't become irrelevant or obsolete because they suffer a loss, or experience an unexpected challenge. They go into a decline because of what they do to themselves like getting stuck in an old pattern, not staying true to what they do best, getting away from their mission, or biting off more than they can chew. Life's hard knocks don't have to be your downfall; in fact, it's often adversity that spurs people and companies on to greatness. They find out their true character when the chips are down and rise to the occasion.

Change is not your enemy — it's your ally. Becoming stale, complacent, stagnant—these options are unworthy of anyone who wants to be unforgettable in business. You can prevent yourself from going there by asking yourself these questions every six months:

- What old ideas can I let go of to experience a renewed approach to work?

- What positive qualities do I need to evolve to stay current and relevant?

- How can I develop those qualities while staying true to my essence?

- What can I do to feed my fire so that I can feel excited about work?

Evolution is essential to a rich and meaningful journey. As you take the first step in a different direction, be patient and compassionate with yourself. Embarking on anything new can be uncomfortable. Pay attention to the signs along the way. You'll know you are on the right path when people and opportunities come into your life to support what's next for you.

When you're on your path to reinventing yourself, things just fall into place.

The Other Side of Crazy

How to keep it together when what's happening at work and in the world is so completely insane.

I used to be so sure I knew the next right step. But, now there is so much uncertainty in business, politics, the environment, the economy, how to parent, the right way to eat— even a positive, self-directed person like myself can feel out of sorts and well, a bit insane.

It's a fact that one in four adults— approximately 57.7 million Americans— experience a mental health disorder in a given year. And I don't have to tell you how scary it is to watch loved ones and co-workers stop being able to deal with the uncertainty.

When everyone is going mad, it's so easy to go down the rabbit hole with them.

When you are on the receiving end of fear and dissatisfaction, it's easy to feel that you're the cause. You may even think that you can cure the anxiety. Forget it! Your job is to take care of yourself so you don't lose it, too.

Here are five essential things you can do right now when people or situations in your life feel out of control.

Call The People Who Love You

Pick up the phone and call someone who gets you and tell the truth. Admit it— your boss is a maniac, your wife is depressed, your son has no direction. You are not perfect, but you are still standing strong. Good for you!

Get Out And Exercise

Healing of the body leads to healing of the mind. That's why every single day you have to do something active, even if it's just walking your dog for 30 minutes. Stop with the excuses already.

Say "Yes" To Opportunity

Don't let people who are unhealthy and out of balance tell you can't do it or make you feel you're not good enough. Say "yes" and go for the promotion, attend networking events, give a speech, host a panel, take the job, and go get that guy. Stop putting your life on hold. You may be avoiding your destiny (and that's crazy).

Stay Open and Find Perspective

The other night at the Dallas airport, I was feeling low. I said to a woman in front of me at the barbeque stand, "I'm not sure I want to go home." She said, "Me neither." I asked her why. She said, "My beautiful son was run over six weeks ago and is now a paraplegic." As I hugged her, I realized my problems were very small.

Be Grateful, Thankful and Satisfied.

My sister and I play a game when we need to remind ourselves of how wonderful life really is. We ask each other these three questions: 1) "What are you grateful for in this moment?" 2) "What are you thankful for?" and 3) "What are you satisfied with?" The answers always clear the clouds away.

When the people we love and those we work for are cracking up, the only path to sanity is to keep working on ourselves.

Hey Tough Cookie, Take A Look At Yourself Before You Crumble

You can't build a positive personal brand on image alone.

Years ago, I struck up a strong business alliance with a woman named Rachel Clark. She was the Senior Vice President of Marketing for a division at Sony that created international television networks. Later, she would hold the same title at The CW. I traveled with her to far-flung places, built successful brands and developed a friendship that has lasted to this day.

I have been fortunate to have many great working relationships with talented women over the almost 19 years I've owned Big Fish. However, there have been times when things didn't go so swimmingly.

Just last month I was enjoying a business lunch in LA with prospective clients when I noticed a disturbing dynamic happening. To my left was the head honcho – a gentleman who was open and interested in working with me. To my right was his top female executive who appeared to be threatened. "Here we go again," I thought.

Like Rachel, some women step into their power with grace— understanding that building a posse of consultants, creative partners and employees can make all the difference. Others go it alone and play the overworked martyr. Still others revel in their chosen role of tough cookie.

Do these women feel that they have to do it all themselves – that if they delegate things will go horribly wrong? Do they think that if they ask for help, they won't be perceived as competent? Or is it that they fear that someone else may shine brighter and they'll be seen as mediocre?

Doing it all yourself makes you look like a worker bee, not a leader. And that isn't the personal brand image you want to project.

Taking on everything with little or no help can give the worker bee job security, but it will only get them promoted to the mid-manager level. There they will languish, never being truly appreciated. Over time, worker bees tend to get sick or downright mean.

You heard me: <u>mean</u>. It comes from the resentment that builds watching others get ahead who seem to not be working as hard. If this feeling is running through your veins, I suggest you get a good mentor or career coach before you start negatively impacting your business and everyone around you.

In terms of your personal brand image, are you a "mean girl gone corporate" or someone inspiring to women?

Perhaps it's not the "I've-got-to-do-this-all-by-myself" belief system that's running women who are mean, maybe it's just their pattern. According to *Psychology Today*, the majority of mean girls do grow up to be mean women. Instead of helping one another build their careers, women sometimes do everything to destroy them.

All across this country, businesswomen complain that their lives are out of balance. Perhaps that's because many working women make more money than their husbands, while still running the household. Overworked and stressed out, they need help. If I'm describing you – little miss overachiever – I encourage you to soften that tough exterior by aligning with people who can lessen your workload and make you look like a star. After all, there's enough meanness and martyrdom in this world... don't you think?

Start today by cultivating a positive personal brand image that's open, not isolated. You'll be seen as a leader among women.

Step 11:
Change Perceptions About You

Every day is a chance to become brand new. If you've been viewed negatively, change perceptions by showing up in your essence and focusing on the unique qualities that make you valuable.

In this step you will learn to:

Change the Conversation

Take Responsibility For Your Reputation

Be In Service Through Volunteering

Climb Out of Your Pigeonhole

Deal With Work Bullies

Change The Conversation And Open Doors

Want to be recognized for your potential? Bust the myths about you.

It's a cold hard truth that conclusions are instantly drawn about you and myths are formed based on assumptions, preconceived notions and first impressions. Any of those myths could be negative. In defense, many of us respond by pointing fingers and carrying a chip on our shoulder, which encourages exclusion. That's one way to go. Another is to give the world a fearless representation of who you are.

Andy Warhol was one of the first major American artists to be open about his homosexuality; and he was criticized for it. He wrote in his book *Popism,* "I decided I just wasn't going to care, because those were all the things that I didn't want to change anyway, that I didn't think I 'should' change... Other people could change their attitudes, but not me." And lo and behold—people did change their *attitudes.*

I had a similar experience while attending the University of Alabama. I found myself confronted by a lot of students who didn't know anyone Jewish, or who had a negative impression of Jews because of prejudice they'd learned at home. In my four years at Bama, I worked to dispel those myths by becoming president of the Jewish sorority and developing its presence on campus in a way that had never been done before.

You can change negative perceptions by proudly accepting yourself.

Maybe everyone sees you a certain way and you want to go in a different direction. Maybe you're the youngest person on your team or the oldest, and you feel invisible. Maybe you're a different color or you come from a different culture. You're a woman in a man's world or a man in a woman's world. Bottom line: you often feel like a fish out of water.

If you are viewed negatively, accept yourself and others will follow. Feeling sorry about your differences will only make people doubt your value. When you're different from the norm, you already attract attention; but the good news is that attracting attention may be the best thing that ever happened to you. Being unique puts you in the spotlight where it's your choice and privilege to shine.

To start busting the myths about you, get out a piece a paper and jot down answers to the following questions:

1) What unique qualities do you have that are advantageous to your company, clients or and/or industry?
2) How are you being pigeonholed because of your differences?
3) How can you turn any negative perceptions about you into positive attributes?

The key to developing self-acceptance (even when you're the only one like you) is to turn your focus toward what you have instead of harboring a sense of scarcity and always looking at what seems to be missing. Comparing yourself to others is the #1 way to sabotage your career. Creating genuine connections and having gratitude for what makes you uniquely *you* goes a long way to turning your differences into your advantage.

No matter who you are, if you are authentic, people will automatically open up to you and feel positively about you.

What Are People Saying About You?

Who you think you are and what others perceive can be two very different things.

Your boss thinks he's the smartest guy in the room. You think he's an idiot. Your assistant boldly asks for a promotion. You think she's got miles to go before she can move up. Your client feels he's right not to change his advertising strategy. You think he just doesn't understand today's market. We all make judgments about the people we work with based on our own perceptions, but how many of us stop to realize that we are also being judged?

So, what are people saying about you? Is there a positive meaning beyond your name? Does that meaning have relevance now? Does your target audience know that you matter in this economy? Can they define the feeling of working with you in a word or phrase? If so, is it how you want to be thought of and valued?

It's time to take responsibility for your reputation, so that you can get your swagger back and stop feeling so unsteady about your longevity in business.

To that end, try to imagine what words come to mind when people say your name. What do people <u>feel</u> when they see you? If you can't answer this question easily, join the club. How can you ever know what someone else is thinking, anyway? And after all, how objective can you really be about yourself?

The story that you tell about yourself is what others will believe. Without that story, they'll make up their own.

You <u>can</u> know what people are thinking about you when you take charge of your perception by shining a light on your talents and unique attributes. I'm not talking about mind control exactly, what I'm talking about is about having a strong influence over how you're perceived by consistently telling a story that's factual, relevant, in service to others and comes from your highest self.

So why should you bother crafting those messages and sharing them with the world? Here's why: to know who you are and be valued for it, to attract what you want, to create demand for your talents, to walk your path with integrity, to distinguish yourself in your chosen field, and make more money doing what you love. Bottom line: when you have a strong value proposition, you'll bust every myth and be seen for your highest potential.

I believe in miracles and destiny, but in the end we make our own reality. The strength of your reputation and the respect you receive begins and ends with you.

What To Do If You've Been Pigeonholed

Trying to squeeze yourself into being something you're not never works.

Being pigeonholed – put into a little box – trust me, it's happened to the best of us. How to get out of that box starts with embracing the values and attributes that make you *you*. By making a list of your talents, passions and unique abilities, then noticing the ways you act in accordance with— and contrary to— those traits you will begin to reinvent yourself and the way others perceive you.

What brand marketing has taught me is that you have to dig deep to uncover what you do differently from your co-workers, your real value and your reason for being. Great brands pour all of this into a verbal and visual container that defines who they are, in a very clear, consistent and authentic way.

The most admired executives and business owners in the world are not slick. They're genuine, innovative, and passionate. Their appeal and magnetism has nothing to do with being someone they're not.

To climb out of your pigeonhole, plant your flag in the ground and declare who you are and what you're good at. If you haven't already done this, I promise that your co-workers, bosses and clients have done it for you. But, they might have gotten it wrong and that's the danger. The good news is it's not too late.

Simply get out a pen and paper and follow these three steps:

1. **Examine Your Values and Passions**
   Make a list of your core values and ask yourself how your actions reflect those values and how they go against them. Then, list what gets you out of bed in the morning and makes time fly at work.

2. **Get Clear On Your Expertise**
   What do you do really well? What are you praised for in the work place? What do you do better than your competitors?

3. **Define What You Want To Be Known For**
   Out of all these talents and strengths, what would you like to be known for that sets you apart for your uniqueness? Write a descriptive paragraph that's loaded with the benefits of working with you. Make sure they support your specialty.

This is the beginning of taking charge of how you're perceived. And your clients/customers/employers will understand EXACTLY what you do, why you do it better than anyone else, and why they need you to do it for them.

By creating a powerful language that defines your value, you can align with the types of projects and people you want to attract.

Is Someone Messing With You At Work?

Here's how To Protect Yourself From Bullies and Saboteurs.

During the last month of 5th grade, my then then-11 year-old daughter shared with us that rumors were being spread about her at school and that her peers were ostracizing her.

Over the years Roxy's teachers would say, "Your daughter is a person who really knows who she is." Now things had drastically changed. When I dropped her off at school, she would ask me to walk her into the classroom. She was frightened of what would be waiting for her.

As adults, many of us have experienced that feeling of uncertainty. We've had co-workers who have spread rumors about us, ignored us or discounted our feelings. Bosses who when giving performance reviews show nothing but displeasure. Competitors who posted negative online reviews of our businesses. Clients who yell at us and bully us into working for less or giving them more *for free.* Now that I think about it, the workplace can be pretty scary!

Sabotage is often fueled by jealousy. In love, jealousy can break your heart. In business, jealousy can kill your career.

Being bullied requires you to go on the offensive – turning the negative attention to your advantage.

When I was pregnant with Roxy, my biggest competitor told *all my clients* that I'd probably be quitting after I had the baby. To combat the speculation, I showed up seven months pregnant at the National Cable Television Association's annual conference with portfolio in hand. I walked the convention floor until my back ached telling everyone that they could count on my company before, during and after the delivery. I picked up six new projects on the spot, and without mentioning my competitor's name. He got branded "out of the loop."

If you have someone who is bullying you or trying to sabotage your career, here are some strategies to help you deal with it.

Change your internal dialogue

You may be asking yourself, "Why me? Do I attract this?" It's time to change your patterns by telling yourself, "I am not a victim and I have choices."

Stand up or you won't stand a chance

When someone is trying to mess with you, go on the offensive. Tell them (and others who matter) the real story. Don't shrink like a violet or push the problem to the side hoping it will go away.

Fight fire with fire

Years ago, when a client yelled at me, I yelled back. My reaction was real and powerful. She got the message that *I wasn't her bitch* and never raised her voice to me again.

Think before you react

If you don't know what to do in the moment, do nothing. Think about the right course of action and take it. Don't go off half-cocked. Listen to your gut and make a plan.

Rally your brand cheerleaders

Make a list of all the people who love you and support your work. Ask them to write positive online reviews and testimonials. Have them make phone calls on your behalf.

When you are being bullied or sabotaged, it's important to honor yourself without expectations. Whether you write a letter or say the way you feel face-to-face, take the necessary action and then let it go. The universe will take care of the outcome.

Like my daughter, you may choose to tell your truth, realize that the environment wasn't really serving you and then leave the situation. (She changed schools and has made wonderful friends.) If you choose to stay, you will have to accept the person as is, forgive them for their past behavior and never trust them fully again.

You simply can't build a successful career on denial. As Oprah once said smartly, "When people show you who they are, believe them."

Why Service Is The Answer

If you're stuck in neutral and you need a new job, then get out of your own way and give back.

I know it seems counter-intuitive, but if you're feeling paralyzed by uncertainty and doubt, my best advice is to resist isolating and get out into your community. Helping find a cure for cancer by running a marathon, volunteering at a local museum, lecturing at a college or industry event, advocating for a worthy cause or mentoring young people will make you look like a leader, someone who has dimension.

Non-profits provide a great platform for strengthening skills and trying out different areas of business. Say you're a research executive, but you've always wanted to try your hand at event planning. Perfect. Volunteer to put on a fundraiser! You may find the experience needed to reinvent yourself and the right people in the room who can help you get into a new career.

When prospective employers or customers learn about your philanthropic nature, they will trust you more.

Getting behind a cause is good for business and makes you look like a hero. In fact, research shows that most Americans would rather do business with brands that are responsible and contribute. The same is true for personal brands. By advocating for a greater good, you will up your own stock and change perceptions.

Case in point, Bill Gates enhanced his personal appeal through his philanthropy. By doing good work to improve education and stop disease in poor nations, he shifted the focus from the negative press accusing Microsoft of being a monopoly to important issues and groundbreaking solutions. Oprah is known for her generosity. U2's Bono and George Clooney are major advocates for fairness and peace. By giving back, they gain respect, admiration and staying power. And so can you.

By channeling your deepest desire to be more than what you are today into something that's going to help others, you'll feel like a million bucks. Bottom line: giving back will make your personal brand more relevant to those in your sphere of influence and that equates to bigger opportunities.

Demonstrate authentic leadership through service. It's instant karma.

At Big Fish, we have been fortunate to work on Nickelodeon's, "Big Green Help", Lifetime's breast cancer awareness campaign, Comedy Central's

"Comedy RX," a hospital-based program promoting the healing powers of laughter, and more. In addition, we give a portion of our billings to The Aquarium of the Pacific and put that fact on every invoice. Our work in the pro-social arena makes us feel good and it makes us look good.

Keep in mind that true advocacy happens at the nexus of integrity and inspiration. In choosing a cause, you should take into consideration your personal values, beliefs and creative ideas and line-up with your company's mission and vision. Here are three questions to ask yourself to help you choose a cause that's right for you:

1) What are you passionate about? Nature, children, art, politics, music..?

2) Which of your talents could be leveraged to make a difference?

3) Is the cause good for your brand? Does it align with where you want to go?

If your business has been going south, or you've lost your job, or you've suffered a set back at work, one sure-fire way to change the negativity around you is to do good work—both on the job and out in the world. Just imagine... the next time someone asks you what you've been up to, you'll have quite an inspiring story to tell.

Giving back is cool and it just happens to be good for your reputation.

Step 12:
Make Peace With
The Past

Self-doubt will always stop you from moving forward. You could be dredging up the muck of your childhood, a bad break-up or a co-worker that went negative on you. Look at it as a gift and stay in the present.

In this step you will learn to:

Rewrite Your Script

Let Go of What Doesn't Work Anymore

Stay Open to the Possibilities

Live In Faith, Not Fear

Is The Past Standing In The Way of Your Future?

On the road to becoming a courageous leader, self-doubt can be the red light that stops you from successfully moving forward.

As I've grown more conscious of my own personal impact, more and more I've taken the right course of action in my business. The problem is, I experience within myself the same old reactions.

Instead of people pleasing and kowtowing to my client, I stand up for my ideas. Instead of meekly waiting for my client to tell me what they think of a new logo concept, I boldly tell them why the change would be good for their business. Instead of playing an agonizing waiting game to receive next steps on a project, I outline a winning strategy.

These are all the moves of a fearless leader. Yet as I take each bold step, I began to doubt myself and question every action. Why? Because everything I'm doing feels unfamiliar and uncomfortable.

When you are in the midst of reinventing yourself, you are transforming into something new and there will be growing pains.

I have vowed to myself to own the place I have earned in the business world. I am stepping into my power knowing that when I'm hired for a project it's because my clients want one of the world's leading brand strategists to guide them to a successful outcome, not be a *yes person.*

Yet, in striving to show up differently, I come face-to-face with my past. I am still the product of an alcoholic mother and a demanding WWII ex-Marine father. Pleasing people and comparing myself to what others think of me is the script of my childhood. It was what I did to survive and fit into the world.

So, do my fish out of water feelings cause me to drift back into old patterns that no longer serve me? No, but oh is it tempting! As a mature professional, I have to rewrite that script in a way that serves me first, and in turn serves my clients. I have to discipline myself to not waver and have faith in the fact that I am awakening to my true nature.

It's not always easy to stay on a path to achieving your highest potential – especially if you've had a difficult childhood or a challenging set of circumstances that have made you question your own value. My knee jerk reaction to any difficult situation is to feel I'm not good enough. When I go there, I start to count my blessings and give gratitude for all that I have and what I've accomplished.

The next time you're struggling, try to take a step back and observe yourself. Whether you're obsessing or wallowing, watch how you get stuck between who you were and who you want to be. I think you'll find that you can't live in those two worlds at once.

Recently, I went to see one of my business coaches. I wanted her to make me feel better about the positive choices I had made (because I felt so lousy). She told me that *my mind* was the only thing standing between where I am today and where I want to go. If I would just let go and have fun — trusting in my process and product, everything positive would flow to me. So that's what I did and that's exactly what happened. Who knew!

It's critical to shift into gratitude the minute you start questioning your self worth.

Make An Anti-Bucket List

Sometimes making peace with the past requires letting go of what doesn't work anymore.

It seems that everyone is making a "bucket list" these days. They want to check off the exciting things they'll do before they die (or kick the bucket). That's nice, but I'd rather make a list of all the things I never want to do again. I call it "My Anti-Bucket List."

1. Hold on to mediocre employees and hope they'll improve
2. Work with a known misogynist
3. Eat wasabi thinking it's avocado
4. Take on a client without a signed contract
5. Beg to stay in a relationship with a client who threatens to fire me (next time, I'll let them)
6. Fly coach to the Middle East
7. Use divisive language to shake things up and create change (come to think of it, maybe "train wreck" wasn't the right word choice)
8. Take on too many clients at the same time
9. Complain about having too many clients at the same time
10. Ski
11. Volunteer to chair a school gala
12. Treat employees like family— I've got one

13. Drink a cocktail in Costa Rica containing ice
14. Work with a client who is having an affair with her boss who happens to be my friend's husband
15. Wear stilettos to a lawn party
16. Work my assistant so hard that she passes out
17. Forget to lock my doors at night
18. Let someone finish the sentence, "I'm saying this as a friend..."
19. Try to grow broccoli in New Mexico
20. Not believe in myself

Before you think about all the places you want to go and all the things you want to do, first decide what you will never do again. Make that list and stick to it.

Life's just too short to repeat what doesn't work for you. So what's on your anti-bucket list?

The Art Of <u>Not</u> Setting Goals Or Making Resolutions

Why staying open— rather than pushing an agenda— could create more abundance.

I'll never forget the time I celebrated New Years' Eve in San Miguel de Allende, Mexico. After an evening of eating tacos, shooting tequila and watching fireworks with good friends, I went to bed thinking about my annual New Years' Day ritual of writing down my accomplishments and setting goals for the new year.

The next morning I woke up, opened my journal and got to work. It all flowed effortlessly until I came to the goal setting section. Try as I may, I couldn't determine revenue targets or project the number of products we'd sell. Frankly, the whole exercise seemed forced.

Maybe my apprehension was due to the fact that my company was about to celebrate its 20th Anniversary or maybe it was because I would also be celebrating a big birthday that year, but for the very first time, I resisted writing down any goals. The expression, "Man plans and God laughs" came to mind.

Letting go, I vowed to be open to the possibilities. Something told me that if I stayed committed to my mission, honed my message and became more visible, I would have a stellar year.

Creating more abundance and attracting opportunities happens when you live your life on purpose.

Yes, it can be a productive exercise to put in writing that you want to earn X amount of dollars or attract a certain client. But let's face it; creating expectations with that kind of specificity is like premeditating disappointment. My advice is to resist the temptation and do the following instead:

1. Uncover your mission and set your intention

2. Write down your dream on paper

3. Learn how to authentically express your desire
4. Craft a marketing plan that builds your brand
5. Get out of your office and in front of key influencers

Dreams come true when you take responsibility for the things you want. Rather than set goals or make resolutions, talk about your mission (the "why" behind what you do) with people who you know will be supportive and those that need what you offer. The more you put your dreams out there, the more powerfully they will be brought back to you in reality.

Let go of the herd mentality of making resolutions and setting specific goals. You'll create more abundance than you could have ever imagined.

Shifting From Fear Into Faith

Faith steps into your consciousness when you accept and adjust your reality to what is.

There is a huge shift happening in the world. What's stirring the unrest inside many of us is a personal desire for transformation and a revolt against the old guard— to take control of our own destiny. People are shouting for more freedom, more balance and more love. Even Mother Nature is shaking things up.

Every day I talk to professionals who are tired of being boxed in, who have jobs that don't make their heart sing, who want to reinvent themselves and their world. Their frustration is real, but their fear of change is realer. And that fear is what keeps them from doing what their heart desires.

Their fear stems from a feeling of scarcity, rather than abundance. It is fueled by attachments to material things and unrealistic expectations about where they *should* be in their career. If your gut is telling you to shift into a new job or fresh way of thinking, but you feel stuck, check yourself and your attachments.

None of us come into the work world with a handbook on how to find our purpose and achieve fulfillment. We simply jump in and do the best we can. But, pushing yourself to keep doing things the same old way when you feel a blinking yellow light inside of you is damaging to your career and your health. It's telling you to pay attention!

So, the next time you feel fear stopping you from embracing the shift happening inside you and out in the world, ask yourself these questions:

What am I thankful for in this moment?

What am I in fear of at this moment?

What do I need to accept about myself?

What do I need to accept about my current situation?

What kinds of changes can I make today?

What changes can I make in the next 90 days?

The first question will calm you down and put you in a happy place. The rest of the questions will move you out of fear, ground you in reality and help you to formulate a plan of action.

In order to move out of fear, you have to identify it. When pangs of anxiety surface, grab pen and paper and describe the source of your distress. Then, visualize yourself making positive changes so you can courageously move past the fear.

Your fear could be something concrete, such as a big work presentation, looming layoffs or a fight with your partner or best friend. Or maybe it's less tangible, say, failure, the disapproval or rejection of others, or the future and what it holds. Naming your fear will help you to manage it and move forward with faith.

The shift is happening. Allow it to unfold and take you to a higher place within yourself, your company, your industry and the world.

About The Author

One of the most sought-after strategists on brand creation and reinvention, Robin Fisher Roffer provides the rocket fuel that has ignited the launch pad of dozens of brands across the globe. Her dynamic spark has unearthed the soul of some of the world's most beloved brands and in turn defined a who's who of successful ventures.

As Founder and CEO of Big Fish Marketing, Robin has crafted brand-building strategies and marketing plans for powerhouse players like A&E, Bloomberg, CNN, NBC Universal, FOX, Food Network, Sony Pictures Television, Verizon and Wet N Wild Cosmetics.

Robin also helps professionals build their personal brands through her books, weekly blog, speeches, workshops and training programs. With a core belief that great brands are built on simple truths, she penned her first book, <u>MAKE A NAME FOR YOURSELF: Eight Steps Every Woman Needs to Create a Personal Brand Strategy for Success.</u>

Her second book, <u>THE FEARLESS FISH OUT OF WATER: How to Succeed When You're the Only One Like You</u> shows professionals how to stay connected and relevant at work while maintaining a unique identity, how to fit in without blending in, and how to transform what's different about you to your advantage.

Utilizing material from her books, Robin develops and leads corporate training programs and workshops for top potentials and sales teams at powerhouse companies like Microsoft, Philips, Mattel, Cox Media, Walmart and UBS. The programs teach executives how to build their own personal brands to create lasting impressions and increase revenue.

An acclaimed speaker and media personality on the topics of career reinvention and personal branding, Robin often keynotes conferences for major corporations, business organizations and universities. She appears as a career expert on national TV and radio shows, and is a contributing career writer for SimplyHired.com.

Prior to Big Fish, Robin was Manager of Creative Services for TNT. There her education in branding went into high gear as she crafted advertising campaigns designed to create awareness for TNT's original movies. Later she directed affiliate-aimed advertising and promotion for CNN, TNT and TBS.

Roffer left Turner in 1992 to start Big Fish Marketing. With her former employer among her first clients, she struck out on her own. Today her client roster includes over 25 media brands, along with companies from the worlds of beauty, energy, insurance and finance.